THE ARTISTIC HOME

THE
ARTISTIC
HOME

DISCUSSIONS WITH ARTISTIC
DIRECTORS OF AMERICA'S
INSTITUTIONAL THEATRES

BY TODD LONDON

INTRODUCTION BY LLOYD RICHARDS

FOREWORD BY PETER ZEISLER

THEATRE COMMUNICATIONS GROUP, INC.

Manufactured in the United States of America

First Edition: February 1988

Library of Congress Cataloging-in-Publication Data

London, Todd.
   The artistic home.

   1. Theater--United States--Planning. 2. Theater--
United States--Production and direction. 3. Theater
management--United States. 4. Theatrical producers
and directors--United States--Attitudes. I. Title.
II. Title: Artistic directors of America's institutional
theatres.
PN2293.P53L66 1988   792'.023'0973   87-33600
ISBN 0-930452-76-3 (pbk.)

ACKNOWLEDGEMENTS

The Artistic Home is a report of TCG's National Artistic Agenda
Project, which is made possible by special grants from the Dayton
Hudson Foundation, the National Endowment for the Arts and The Pew
Charitable Trusts.

TCG wishes to thank American International Group, and Edward E.
Matthews, Executive Vice President-Finance of American International
Group and President of the McCarter Theatre Board of Trustees, for
hosting the New York City meeting.

TCG also wishes to thank the following theatres for hosting regional
meetings: Alliance Theatre, Berkeley Repertory Theatre, Center Stage,
Eureka Theatre Company, Goodman Theatre, Mark Taper Forum, and Yale
Repertory Theatre.

CONTENTS

INTRODUCTION

In 1985 a group of theatre trustees asked their own artistic
directors a wonderfully explosive question: Beyond money and
survival, what do you want — what is your vision, and what will it
take to get you there? The question was an invitation to fantasy,
but also a challenge to scrutinize fantasy and demonstrate the
artistic reality in our rhetoric.

The question provoked us all. We sought a format of dialogue, a way
of sharing thoughts, fears, concerns, hopes, inadequacies — and
even visions — with one another. The essence of those meetings, to
the degree that it can be distilled, is contained in this report:
These are the dreams of artistic people, pragmatically formulated
into recognizable formulae for action.

There is, in fact, no one vision for the nonprofit theatre. Art,
fortunately, does not arrange itself so neatly. But this collection
of statements does reveal that the tremendous surge of artistic
energy and daring which forged, established and validated the
nonprofit theatre movement in this country more than 25 years ago
still exists. Almost three generations later, the questions and
problems are different. But individually, there exists a
restlessness which can be sensed in these pages and which attests to
the prospect of determined, considered and projectable growth.

The challenge was issued. The visions are revealed. It is left
only to act.

-- Lloyd Richards

FOREWORD

By Peter Zeisler

Throughout its 27-year history, Theatre Communications Group has been committed to nurturing equally the artistic growth and the financial stability of the nonprofit professional theatre in this country. At no time in the field's evolution has the issue of maintaining a healthy balance between these priorities been more critical than now, as the nonprofit theatre struggles to ensure not only its institutional survival, but its future as a vital art form.

The Artistic Home: Discussions with Artistic Directors of America's Institutional Theatres was born out of a challenge. The challenge came from a group of trustees attending TCG's 1985 National Symposium in Costa Mesa, California. Entitled "Taking the Next Step," the conference was a gathering of nearly 200 representatives of theatres across the United States, who came together to explore how to take the next step in the evolving partnership among artistic directors, managers and trustees, and how best to alleviate what has been called the "artistic deficit" in their producing organizations — a term invented several years ago to describe the condition that prevails when economic priorities begin to take precedence over aesthetic concerns.

For the first time, theatre trustees were extremely vocal about the need for clarification of their theatres' artistic visions, goals and needs — the basic tools required for trustees to function effectively as public partners in a theatre's leadership and as zealous advocates for their theatres' artistic missions in their communities. These trustees made it clear that artists were not communicating their needs clearly or often enough to their boards, and they called upon TCG to work with the nation's artistic directors to develop a "national agenda" for the American theatre, in which artistic needs and goals would be articulated. Only then, they contended, could board members function effectively in today's competitive fund-raising climate. One trustee told the artists and managers present, "Funds can be raised if we know why they are needed."

And so, it was at the behest of these trustees that the National Artistic Agenda Project began, but it began where it had to — with the artistic directors — for any other route would surely end in compromised visions.

The project is the most extensive initiative of its kind ever undertaken in this country and represents the first time the theatre's artistic leaders nationwide have come together to assess the past, present and future of the nonprofit professional theatre. It comes at a crucial time in the evolution of the field, as the nonprofit professional theatre movement enters its second quarter-century, when its founders' dreams are beginning to intersect with the visions of new generations of artistic leadership. The pioneering phase is over; today, theatres exist throughout the country. Buildings have been built or remodeled to house them. Quite a few organizations have entered their second -- or even third -- stage of artistic leadership. And, many communities now take for granted the presence of "their" theatres as integral parts of the cultural landscape.

The principal question to be addressed in the coming years concerns the degree of growth for these theatres. Are they going to serve primarily a presenting function, or will they be institutions that explore and nurture art? If it is going to be the latter, much more attention needs to be paid, as this report stresses, to the needs of the creative and interpretive artists — starting with the artistic director him or herself.

The nonprofit theatres in this country "grew like Topsy." There were no role models; there was no appropriate frame of reference upon which to base the new concept of a decentralized, professional, noncommercial theatre. The founders of the movement spent more than two decades launching these theatres, putting the institutional structures in place and ensuring their tenuous survival; now it is high time to consider what it would take to enable them to flourish artistically. In one sense the theatres were victims of their own success; they had become so good at making do with what they had — even excelling within those parameters — and so adept at making art "efficient," that they had lost the ability to stand back and look at what their artistic resources could — or should — be. Despite an impressive record of achievement, nearly everyone agreed that the gap between what had been achieved and the potential for future achievement had never been greater. The first step toward effecting change was to examine the structures and working conditions that had been developed around the art, and to evaluate the artistic prospects for the future.

The resulting series of nationwide meetings has provided a unique forum for candid and sincere sharing, collaborative probing, creative questioning, agile brainstorming and more than a little self-criticism. Artistic directors asked tough questions of themselves — and of each other. Notwithstanding the enormous progress the nonprofit professional theatre had made in its relatively short lifetime, there was an absence of complacency in these meetings, and a willingness on the part of artistic directors to take responsibility for the current state -- and future progress — of the field. Yes, they admitted, artistic compromises are being made; but they did not take the easy route of blaming problems solely on a lack of money.

Reading The Artistic Home is like walking in on a high-powered brainstorming session that began hours before, and then leaving in the middle of it. You don't know what came before or what will come after, but you can feel the immediate intensity of the proceedings. Todd London's report is by no means a transcript, but rather an attempt to convey in writing the essence of discussions that took place over a total of 17 days, to reveal the process behind those deliberations, and to synthesize the major themes, issues and examples gleaned from a dizzying array of topics discussed by the artistic directors of America's nonprofit professional theatres.

The project has engendered an impressive compilation of innovative ideas, identified mutual concerns and shared solutions. This report allows these ideas and concerns to be shared now with other artists, managers and trustees, as well as with the public.

The report provides a rare glimpse of the American theatre through the eyes of its artistic leaders and serves as a point of departure for further discussions. The discussions offer insights into the complex issues that confront the highly diverse noncommercial theatre field today. As John Dillon, artistic director of the Milwaukee Repertory Theater, put it: "Lurking between the lines of the report is a description of our theatres — not the public relations kind of description artistic directors are usually called upon to give, but something more real."

The purpose of the report is to raise questions, foster ongoing interchange and act as a catalyst to assist theatres in their own artistic long-range planning, as well as to encourage each theatre to use the fruits of the deliberations to suit its own particular needs and circumstances, and to seek the most appropriate solutions for its unique situation. The size and diversity of the American theatre, as well as the tremendous variety in repertoires, preclude any uniform panacea. There are no universal answers. The word "agenda" should therefore not be misperceived -- it is used here in the sense of a list of topics for discussion, as in a meeting agenda, rather than as a specific plan for action. This agenda is to be pursued, not followed.

Responsibility for the use of the paper, and for its potential to help create change, finally rests with the leaders of theatres all over the country. The collective actions of these individual theatres, each having made its own adaptations, will produce a new national agenda for American theatre, from which, it is hoped, adequate support for real artistic growth will be generated.

One of the most important results of the meetings has been to bring into focus the debilitating effects of isolation on artists — a byproduct of the field's successful decentralization, which has often left artistic directors to cope alone or on a local basis with artistic matters of national importance and applicability. Despite the revolution in jet travel and satellite hookups, communication is still difficult in a country that itself is almost a continent.

For this reason, I hope the National Artistic Agenda Project will serve as the beginning of an ongoing process of exchange among theatre practitioners, trustees and audiences about what is required if we are to forge first-rate art in our theatres. At a meeting of the TCG board of directors, Garland Wright, artistic director of the Guthrie Theater cautioned, "Like theatre, these discussions cannot be trapped in time. What is important is that the conversation be ongoing, so that the moment keeps existing in the present tense. By sharing our thoughts, our thoughts keep changing."

By identifying and analyzing the issues currently impeding artistic growth, TCG expects the report to make a strong case for such change -- and tc underscore why change must occur on a continuing basis if theatre is to be a vital art form. That vitality is the only way to assert the importance of theatre to the cultural fabric of this nation.

THE ARTISTIC HOME

INTERIOR WALLS: THE LIMITS OF IMAGINATION

"More than anything, I want a bigger, broader, more
active imagination."
                    -- Fontaine Syer
                    Artistic Director
                    Theatre Project Company

Imaginations create theatres. Before money is raised or space
found, before boards are assembled or business systems structured,
someone asks "what if?" and a theatre is born. This "what if?" is the
primary question, the one that has brought a community of over 250
American theatres into existence during the past few decades and made
that network the country's largest employer of theatre artists. These
two words are the source of the thousands of new plays written,
productions mounted and performances enacted across the country every
year, representing a range of work unthinkable even 20 years ago. It is
the question these artists always come back to, even after the building
is built, the subscription brochure mailed, the grant requested and the
play reviewed. "What if?" precedes everything, including the first
expression of need: "If only (we had)..."

Naturally, then, it was to the quality of their own imaginations
that artistic directors first turned while evaluating the current state
of their work in nonprofit theatres. In order to make better theatre
within the institutions, these directors agreed, they need, more than
anything, better imaginations and more opportunities to activate what they
imagine. This fundamental equation between the quality of work and the
quality of imagining came up throughout the TCG meetings, where many
artistic directors expressed the desire to go beyond what they see as a
plateau they have reached in their art; following the theatrical boom and
struggle for survival over the past decades, many artistic directors feel
that they've attained a certain consistency in the quality of their work,
but that the level of that work is still not high enough. Some want to
do wilder work; others more playful. Some envision a more human, less
technological theatre. Others believe theatre has to keep up with
technology. Some want to work on a larger scale. Some want to simplify.
All want to make better theatre. All want to ask more exciting "what
ifs?" and then turn their imaginings into realities, from "if only" into
"what we're doing now...."

Certainly, the difficult struggles theatres face in order to survive
can constrict the imaginations of those working within them. As Lloyd
Richards has argued, aiming at the stars and constantly hitting the
streetlights can be enervating for the artistic process. The search for
economical, small-cast single-set plays, for example, can discourage
playwrights from thinking beyond those limitations and encourage artistic
directors to eliminate options, such as producing two large-scale plays
in the same season, before these options are even entertained. "I'm not
even programmed to dream the dream the way European directors do," one
artistic director argued, referring to the scale of her work. Necessity,

1

artistic directors feel, often dictates vision, instead of the other way around.

Although the realities of survival in the theatre can constrict the imagination in this way, many artistic directors, faced with the limitations of their work, seem almost eager to point the accusing finger at themselves. Their problems, they say, are of their own making. The restrictions of what they sometimes feel is a "sausage factory" approach to production, in which various projects with unique needs tend to get cranked or churned or carted out as if each were the same as every other, are essentially self-imposed. "Things don't happen the way they should for purely interior reasons," a Chicago area artistic director argued. "I can't think of many obstacles in my way that I haven't put there myself or that I couldn't remove if I only had more time to work problems out." Again and again, the artistic leaders of the country's nonprofit theatres assailed themselves for insufficient use of imagination, lack of courage to insist unyieldingly on following their personal visions of what the theatre should be and failure to reenvision more exciting ways of making theatre. With more time and greater artistic resources, including expanded artistic staffs, they believe, it will become possible to overcome their interior limitations and move the theatres' work to a new level of excellence.

1. __Artistic Directors need time for thought, study and reflection,__
__separate from their day-to-day producing responsibilities.__

Imagination and vision can't be bought, nor can they be produced on demand. Yet artistic directors expect themselves to provide both on a regular basis in a system whose deadlines, administrative responsibilities and continuous demand for "product" cut deeply into time required for thought, study, research and reflection. Some artistic directors split their work day between office and home, in order to balance the need to focus on their personal artistic work and the need to keep involved with the workings of the theatre institution. Unfortunately, time out of the office can easily be misunderstood by people who equate real work with being in the office. An artistic director, talking about the value of spending her mornings working at home, away from her staff's constant need for attention, related an anecdote about one such misunderstanding. She received a call from a staff member one day around 11:30 a.m. The caller, convinced that what qualifies as work happens only in an office, apologized for calling her boss at home, saying "I hope I didn't wake you." Some artistic directors look forward to stretches of time away from the theatre as the periods during which the bulk of their thinking, planning, studying and script reading happen without interruption. A group of artistic directors, who had traveled out of their theatres' regions to the TCG meeting, thanked TCG for giving them an opportunity to get away from the phone and onto a plane, where, they unanimously agreed, their best work seems to get done.

The need for time away from the day-to-day demands of producing stems from a fundamental schizophrenia in the lives of American artistic directors, especially those who are primarily directors. The institutional functions of their work as producers often directly contradict their needs as artists. As one artistic director put it: "As producer, I must be a decisive catalyst for action; organized, extroverted, nurturing, people-pushing and competent, keen to the administrative details of marketing, development, sales and real estate. As director, when I'm making a play of my own, I must remain sensitive, inward-directed, vulnerable, even ambiguous. Each of these sides suffers at the hands of the other."

Artistic directors differ about which parts of this split they prefer. There are many who enjoy balancing the two sides of the job, even though their need to protect the artistic side tends to grow as the institutional demands increase. Others, who don't direct, prefer to function primarily as producers. Still others produce because they think it is the only realistic means of creating a body of work as directors in this country. This large group fantasizes a different relationship to the institution, as one such director explained. "I would -- ideally and unrealizably -- dream of being a freelance director in my own theatre. I want to get up in the morning and, like a painter, go into my studio and paint my painting, but, unlike that painter, I also have to run a gallery in order to do it."

Although overcoming the internal obstacles which keep the imagination in check is the ultimate responsibility of each artistic director, the theatre's staff and board can help them carve out the time and space necessary to the process of advancing an artistic vision. Essentially, this need can be addressed through scheduling. Artistic directors require schedules allotting daily, weekly and yearly time out of the office to read and think generally, as well as time to see other work, study, prepare and read for specific projects at the theatre. Their schedules need to remain flexible enough, they agree, to accommodate different sets of needs and expectations when they are also directing. Furthermore, artistic directors would benefit from a schedule that allows for more advance time to plan projects in collaboration with other artists, thereby expanding time for creative thinking and gestation, while cutting down on the pressures of last-minute planning. Every project requires its own amount of preparation, artistic directors believe, whether that translates into months, years or, as in the case of one highly successful recent production, a decade of thought, research and planning.

Many artistic directors also suggest that long-range schedules provide sufficient time for artistic sabbaticals. Six-month or one-year stretches away from the theatre can be necessary for artistic directors to study and re-charge themselves by seeing other work and exploring related interests, as well as rest and recuperation. Artistic directors refer to universities as a fair model for professional sabbaticals, where professors are entitled every seven years to 12 months of paid leave (at a salary level that makes it possible for them to live during that period without taking outside work) to pursue research, writing and outside projects. A number of artistic directors who have already taken such sabbaticals have found the time invaluable in that it enabled them to refocus aesthetic priorities and adjust long-term plans. Certainly, the renewed energy and clarity of vision which can result from a sabbatical benefits the theatre as a whole. Similarly, occasional short-term leaves to direct at other theatres can revitalize artistic directors, in addition to cutting down on their feelings of isolation and giving them the opportunity to observe other theatres at work. Moreover, artistic directors believe that this time away adds to the longevity of artistic directors by diminishing the potential for "burn out."

2. **Artistic directors need more consistent involvement with other artists to nourish their own creative thinking and encourage their personal visions.**

Above all else, artistic directors say they share a sense of isolation. The demands of their individual theatres, their personal work as artists and their responsibilities to their local communities keep them too absorbed to see productions at other theatres, to communicate regularly with peer artistic directors or to stay informed about the work of independent theatre artists, especially those whose work is less visible or familiar to them. One New York artistic director said that, despite her best intentions, she speaks with artistic directors of similar theatres -- including friends and colleagues within the city -- only once every year or two, usually at the TCG National Conference. Others feel that distance isolates them; lack of contact with exciting and influential theatre across the country or around the world can keep them from challenging their own assumptions about what is possible in the theatre. One artistic director put on his "wish list" an open air travel pass, to allow him easy and last-minute access to theatres in other cities.

Most important, artistic directors acknowledge that the growth of complex institutional structures has insulated them more and more from individual artists, the lifeblood of the theatres. An artistic director who founded a theatre as a home for artists may now have precious little time to spend outside of rehearsal with writers, actors, directors or designers. Artistic directors have observed a growing rift between individual unaffiliated artists and the theatre institutions. This situation has created a kind of loneliness that can pervade the institution, where the artistic head, who plans and guides the theatre towards the creation of a body of work, feels cut off from the theatre's heart: the fellow artists who give life to that work.

The artistic directors who came together to discuss these issues all have different aesthetic concerns; they all have different visions of the work they want to pursue. Some passionately believe that only by supporting our living, native playwrights can we create a truly contemporary theatre. Others, more director-centered, think the wave of the future is adventurous, large-scale experimentation with classics. Some worry that today's "event mentality" in marketing, which tries to turn each play into a once-in-a-lifetime offering, is making the straightforward interpretation of intimate plays seem dull. Some see the spoken word as the essential medium of theatre; others care more about the language of design. Whatever their vision, many of these artists are forced, within their theatres, to articulate it alone, without the support of other like-minded artists. In fact, the artistic director is often a theatre's only fulltime artistic staff member, even in

4

organizations with sizable administrative staffs. This isolated position within the institution creates an unrealistic demand on individuals who, in addition to continually exploring, redefining and deepening their own visions, must constantly verbalize them for the theatre's staff, trustees and community; defend them against attacks; and sell them to the world-at-large. This burden increases under the strain of artistic isolation.

Many artists believe that without additional artistic support, their visions, and the work they produce, get watered down until theatres come to resemble each other, and eccentricity, one of the theatre's most attractive features, vanishes from the stage. Without exception, artistic directors feel the need for the support of other artists. Increased support, it has been suggested, can be found inside and outside the institution. Many theatres have appointed associate artistic directors for just this purpose: to share the artistic responsibilities and help artistic directors balance the theatre's long-term development work with its day-to-day production activity. This support might also come in the form of a resident company of actors or individual writers, designers, directors or dramaturgs on staff, involved in ongoing discussions about the work. Or support might take the shape of artists on the board of trustees to help articulate the theatre's work and, so, relieve the artistic director from the sole responsibility of fulfilling and defending the theatre's vision. Associate or resident artist positions offer another means of supporting the development of unique visions and nourishing creative thinking. These individuals, with a partial time commitment to a particular institution, usually perform tasks related to their expertise for that theatre, while the salary or stipend they receive supports their own creative work in or outside of it.

Short-term retreats with other artists or artistic directors to work on projects without the demands of production and the use of outside artistic directors as guest directors are other methods theatres have explored to reduce artistic isolation. Co-productions or productions shared between theatres, which will be discussed later on, can also help bring artistic directors together and get them into other theatres. For artistic directors who are not directors, the need to have artists around may be even greater. One such artistic director expressed a need for artistic teams of directors, designers and writers with whom to discuss his plans. Whatever the form, the purpose is the same: to help provide inspiration and courage -- encouragement -- to the artistic leaders of the theatre and to ease their isolation through ongoing dialogue with people who share their concerns and speak their language.

3. Artistic directors need more interaction with other disciplines and fields.

Even though theatre depends on collaboration between different kinds of artists, the writers, composers, choreographers, performers and designers involved rarely come from or work outside of the field. As a group -- with the possible exception of a growing number of theatre directors who have recently begun working in opera -- these artists tend to be isolated from the other arts and humanities; as a profession,

5

theatre often verges on insularity. Artistic directors speculate that this isolation results from theatre's unique position as the one art form that most ambivalently straddles the line between art and popular entertainment. Some, feeling out of touch with the leading edges of other disciplines, worry that theatre too often lags behind the rest of the arts and humanities. Study of and involvement with related fields, they believe, would help revitalize theatre and strengthen its position within the culture.

Crossover between disciplines might take many forms. For some artistic directors it simply means having more time to keep current, to research and study outside of theatre. For others it means involving people from various walks of life in the process of making theatre, especially in the research phases of specific projects. Before the Goodman Theatre (Chicago) began rehearsing David Mamet's Glengarry Glen Ross, cast members spent two weeks with groups of salesmen, learning their sales pitches and tactics. Teams of actors and salesmen then practiced these techniques on each other. The Theatre Project Company's (St. Louis) cast spent 10 days in two local high schools with students, teachers and counselors in order to develop a rough scenario for a piece about teenage pregnancy. As simple or obvious as these specific research tools might seem, they are examples of what current rehearsal processes -- with limits on time and money -- rarely allow to happen. Likewise, theatres often need specific theatrical expertise for individual projects, such as dialect and speech coaches and movement instructors.

Less project-directed involvement with other fields of endeavor is equally desirable. Bringing specialists from other disciplines onto a theatre's staff can expand the frame of reference for creating new projects. When Peter Hall took over the Royal Shakespeare Company, for instance, he hired a social historian to augment his staff, relate the company's work to the culture around it and open new areas of exploration. One of the great success stories of modern translation occurred when the American theatre invited the poet Richard Wilbur into its fold, a collaboration which produced some of the best English-language Moliere translations to date. Chicago theatres keep in regular contact with Tribune critic Richard Christiansen, who, because of his own extensive travel, can serve as a valuable resource for finding out about important work happening in other parts of the theatrical world. This connection seems natural in a community where the journalist, along with politicians, blues, jazz and folk musicians, and sports figures, is so integral to the life and history of the city. The Mark Taper Forum (Los Angeles) actually brought the critical voice on staff to challenge the theatre from inside when they appointed a local drama critic dramaturg, as Great Britain's National Theatre had done so successfully with Kenneth Tynan in the 1950s.

Closer contact with roots of a theatre's community can be a by-product of collaboration across disciplinary lines. Another appointment at the Mark Taper Forum filled the position of associate artistic director with a trained anthropologist. This addition incorporated a different perspective into the artistic direction of the theatre and introduced research and marketing methods outside the ken of press agents, making it possible for the theatre to reach and develop potential audiences in non-theatregoing communities. These efforts significantly changed the cultural mix of the theatre's audience for the first time by attracting large numbers of people from Los Angeles's sizable Hispanic community for the company's production of Zoot Suit by Luis Valdez. Certainly, this kind of collaboration might include any number of other fields, from psychology to anthropology to sculpture, from sports to politics to religion -- as in the case of one theatre which involves in audience discussions of its productions a rather fanatical priest who fires people up and forces them to look at the racial assumptions in their work.

Certainly, there are other, less formal ways for artistic directors and theatre staffs to interact with people from different fields. Many involve the allocation of time and money in limited ways. Many artistic directors would value, for example, the time to attend seminars and conferences, and to include papers and journals in their daily reading. Some theatres initiate symposia on topics relating to the theatre's work, which involve experts from outside disciplines. Some add professionals from other art forms or humanities to boards of trustees and advisory committees. Whatever the form, most artistic directors agree that these collaborations with artists and experts from other fields of endeavor, project-oriented or nonspecific, brief or longterm, can only enrich the theatre and make it a more vital, relevant part of the culture.

MAKING ROOM IN THE HOUSE: LOOKING FOR NEW FLEXIBILITY

IN OLD STRUCTURES

"Maybe institutional theatre is the one inflexible
thing in this variable world."

-- Mark Lamos
Artistic Director
Hartford Stage Company

If the "wish lists" artistic directors carried to TCG meetings in
their heads had been written down, one word would have appeared almost
everywhere: "flexibility." More flexible schedules, they wished for, and
flexible rehearsal processes, flexible previews, flexible subscription
series, flexible budgets and flexible programming. As well as any, that
word encompasses their diverse artistic needs. Even the institutional
structures which work most of the time can, artistic directors find, have
difficulty accommodating change. The value of the subscription season,
for example, is enormous; it gives theatres a financial base of security
which allows them to plan ahead and guarantee audiences for all shows,
even those with more limited appeal, thus cutting their dependence on
reviews for getting bodies in the seats. In fact, artistic directors
almost unanimously believe that the benefits of subscription outweigh the
drawbacks. And yet, for all its advantages, subscription can create for
the theatres a kind of inflexibility in scheduling that artistic
directors feel the need to counter. Subscription is just one area into
which artistic directors want to build more flexibility. The current
rehearsal process, performance schedules which severely limit previews
and make dates for opening seem inexorable and the standard manner of
putting a season together are others. Overall, most artistic directors
believe that the best methods of making theatre within the institutions
are the most flexible ones.

In the process of putting a theatre season together, the need to
make changes in either the season itself or a particular rehearsal
process is often pre-empted by non-artistic concerns. The cost of
keeping subscribers informed about scheduling changes, for instance, made
it increasingly difficult for one artistic director to revise the
schedule at all. "We used to send out mailings to our subscribers five
times a year, announcing our plans for the season and any changes we
needed to make. Now we can only afford one mailing, which makes schedule
changes almost impossible." This story is not unusual. Subscription
marketing has accustomed audiences to buy in order to see specific
productions, rather than to underwrite (literally sub-scribe) the
theatre's costs by paying in advance for anything it produces. While
many theatres have bought time to finalize season plans by advertising

8

some slots as "TBA" (To Be Announced), these non-decisions up front can cost more down the road. Indeed, any change at all, under the current subscription structures, usually costs money. In this way, a program that has made the growth of institutional theatres possible can sometimes serve to restrict the artistic process within.

A few theatres have found creative ways of side-stepping the rigid decision-making process that sometimes accompanies subscription. The New York Shakespeare Festival customarily announces its plans project by project. Subscribers (or in this case passholders) buy into the theatre's overall vision without always knowing what they will see, until a particular project, considered by the theatre ready to go into production, is announced. Other theatres prepare a subscription series well ahead of time and then produce or present (by bringing in other theatre or related arts events) a second season, which they sell as it is lined up. Berkeley Repertory Theatre (Berkeley, Calif.), for example, operates a "parallel season," producing individual projects and co-productions in uniquely suited spaces throughout the San Francisco Bay area. Second seasons, like this one, can allow a theatre to present different types of work from what it might offer to subscribers and, by doing so, diversify its artistic program.

1. <u>More flexible subscription plans and performance schedules could accommodate a variety of developmental needs and changing artistic requirements within a season.</u>

"I dream of selling subscriptions for a hundred-plus dollars, with no titles and no dates -- just the promise to deliver a full season of our best work." This artistic director's dream is shared by many, but it is one that has little grounding in current subscription realities. In order to sell subscriptions, season planning needs to be done way in advance, often in the heat of the preceding season. So, without the opportunity to evaluate the present season, sometime in the middle of production or even while directing a play, an artistic director must pin down a large number of variables -- rights to a play or the potential readiness of a play in the process of development, actor commitments, directors' schedules, to name a few -- on at least four and usually more projects that will go into the following season's offering. Often these projects must be negotiated, planned and developed over a period of years, and the chances of them falling into place for the deadline of a subscription brochure are slim.

Because the process of cultivating projects for the theatre is slow and variable, with each project requiring a different gestation period, and because the deadlines of subscription can be inexorable, decisions get made before they are ready, and potential successes become possible failures in the hurry. Seasons are, thus, viewed as things "picked," into which plays are "slotted," rather than as carefully developed parts of the theatre's total body of work.

9

Once these slots are created and sold, they tend to lock theatres into a mode of production that lacks the room for maneuvering. Like a row of dominoes, the plays in a season each have something lined up before and behind them with little or no space between; trying to move one can upset the whole season. The season, once begun, rolls on without opportunity for the theatre to capitalize on its successes or bury its failures. A well-received show usually has no ability to extend its run more than the one or two weeks some schedules allow. This can mean loss of revenue and new audiences. If a show is less successful artistically or less popular with single-ticket buyers, it usually has to continue the run through the end, in order to accommodate the pre-sold subscription audience (even if a theatre tries to fill the first weeks of a run with subscribers, there are always those who have exchanged tickets for nights later on). In this way a theatre's best and worst efforts get equal weight and visibility, a situation which undercuts attempts to present individual projects as distinct, special works.

The rotating repertory system, initially aspired to by many of America's institutional theatres, has one built-in solution to this dilemma: successful productions remain in the repertory, and unsuccessful ones don't. The fact that a theatre can maintain a show's life by keeping it in rotation with others also gives special emphasis to those productions best representing the theatre by keeping them going -- as in the case of many European theatres -- for years. Thus, productions of dense or difficult plays gain the opportunity to mature over time. Worthy productions with limited audience appeal still get an airing, on a schedule commensurate with the size of the potential audience. The failures get buried, thus creating a body of work primarily represented by those projects the theatre can take pride in and be supported by. By spreading the runs of shows out over a longer span of time, rep gives word-of-mouth a chance to get around and eases the burden of having to get everyone who might want to see the work into the theatre within the first few weeks. The rotating rep system allows for a theatre's developmental work or projects of a more esoteric nature to be supported by the revenues from productions with popular appeal. It also enables theatres to continue work on a play during the course of its long run.

There are some American theatres that do all or some of their work in rep. Whether the repertory runs year-round or for part of the season, theatres working this way must maintain resident acting ensembles -- often large ones -- during its course. American Repertory Theatre (Cambridge, Mass.), American Conservatory Theatre (San Francisco) and Jean Cocteau Repertory (New York City) have been able to produce entire seasons in rep by developing either full resident companies or core ensembles. Some small artist collectives or experimental ensembles, like the Wooster Group (New York City) and the San Francisco Mime Troupe, who develop their work together over a long period of time are able to keep their complete body of work in repertory, available for revivals or touring. The Acting Company (New York City), which tours almost exclusively, presents all of its work in repertory during nationwide tours.

For theatres which prefer to work without resident acting companies, there are countless variations on rotating repertory. (Some of the pros and cons of resident companies will be discussed in Chapter III.) Staggione rep, common in opera, is a modified repertory, in which the season is divided into two or three partial seasons, each of which offers a limited rotation of two or three productions. The Mark Taper Forum (Los Angeles) runs an annual mini-repertory, consisting of two plays chosen for their relationship to one another. The reasoning behind the event centers more on artistic impact than on scheduling concerns; performed side-by-side like this, these plays gain a new kind of resonance in contradistinction to each other. Center Stage (Baltimore) has undertaken another variation on the subscription package that incorporates the flexibility of rep into an otherwise typical subscription season and which sells a program instead of individual plays, giving the theatre more lead time and flexibility in the final selection. The "Re:discovery" series will supplant the sixth production of Center Stage's season with three plays, drawn from new writing, contemporary drama and lesser-known classics, presented in rotating repertory. Because the offer actually raises the theatre's offerings from six to eight, it can be sold as a special program even before the announcement of specific titles. It will allow the theatre to explore a variety of work -- more work -- at less risk, since no single show will carry the burden of an entire mainstage run. Moreover, it is an example of subscription style programming that avoids for part of the season the trap of plugging a play into a slot. A few theatres are exploring limited rep situations like this one, in which one slot in a season will be split between two or three plays.

A familiar model from the commercial theatre, the straight run, might be beneficial for some theatres, but it is hard to adopt within the subscription season. Here a play runs as long as it has an audience because there is no next production scheduled in the same space. Nonprofit theatres commonly adopt a modified form of this open run at the end of the season; they schedule plays with strong popular appeal in the final slot with the hope that they can run all summer long. Theatres with second spaces are sometimes able to move a successful production to another stage, although it is unusual for a theatre to have two stages similar enough to allow for movement between them without requiring extensive design and staging alterations. Theatres, such as those in New York City and Chicago, with proximity to commercial venues can sometimes produce or co-produce a nonprofit or commercial transfer of a successful production. In tight real estate markets, the lack of available space or space of a proper size can make such transfers problematic. Moreover, this is a separate, complicated procedure, demanding extra financing and often creating lag time between closing and the opening of the extension, a crack through which many of the virtues of an original mounting can fall.

Successful shows can, however, also enjoy prolonged life when picked up by another nonprofit theatre or by a theatre festival. In fact, theatres have lately been exploring the advantages of regional tours among nonprofits as a way of extending the life of a production. In the case of <u>Fences</u>, perhaps the most dramatic recent example of this kind of tour or production sharing, the production began at Yale Repertory Theatre (New Haven, Conn.), continued after a year's hiatus with the original cast and production team at the Goodman Theatre (Chicago), and moved to another run at Seattle Repertory Theatre before previewing commercially in San Francisco and settling into a long, award-winning run on Broadway. This "tour" not only provided a longer run, but expanded the audience and allowed the creative team several full rehearsal periods to further the production's development.

A process like that of <u>Fences</u> provides creators with something the rigidity of the subscription season, unlike lengthy repertory runs, too often squeezes out of the schedule: time to work on a show once it has been in front of an audience. In spite of the fact that nearly all artistic directors believe that previews and rehearsals during previews are the most valuable periods in the development of a production, both are a rare commodity in the institutional theatre. Many theatres have only a few -- between two and five -- previews before official openings and press nights. They feel they can't afford more. The reduced ticket prices and extra time without reviews (on which single-ticket sales often depend) on top of the time the theatre must remain dark in order to mount the physical production bring in less income than regular ticket sales after press coverage. And yet in spite of all these fiscally sound reasons for shorter previews, the artistic directors find the work suffering for lack of opportunity to incorporate the discoveries made in performance. The artists begin to feel as if they're operating under the pressures of stock company scheduling, regularly opening shows before they're ready. In addition, insufficient previews can be damaging to the artists who are often reviewed after too little time in front of an audience.

Almost all artistic directors believe that current attitudes toward previews need to be turned around. Too often, they feel, previews are approached as part of the performance schedule; rather, they argue, previews are first and foremost, an integral part of the rehearsal process, as important as the part of rehearsal that takes place without an audience, in which initial staging and scene development get done.

Certainly, changing the prevailing mindset about previews is not easy. This is one artistic concern that clearly stems from financial considerations. Theatres would have to shoulder the additional costs; newspapers would have to accept later deadlines for reviews; and independent directors and designers, whose schedules are already over-full, would have to be available to stay longer in residence. Moreover, current union-management agreements would have to be renegotiated to allow expanded rehearsal hours during previews and after opening. One artistic director expressed the desire many feel to continue working on a show during its run, saying "I'm as interested in the final performance as the first." Sometimes, however, artistic directors find actors unwilling to rework a show after it has been reviewed.

Artistic directors believe that the need for additional previews is

pressing enough -- the difference in rehearsal hours alone for a show
with two previews and one with a week of previews is substantial -- to
try to effect a change. Three Chicago area theatres have already found
different ways of adding previews. Northlight Theatre valued additional
previews so much that it took time from the pre-audience rehearsal period
to add some. Remains Theatre scheduled a full rehearsal day (with no
performance) after three previews and a day off, to provide the time to
work into a show necessary improvements. Goodman Theatre has shown that
by making this time a priority, by carefully scheduling days off,
matinees and openings, and by selling to subscribers the theatre's
dedication to process, as many as 10 to 13 previews are possible within
-- and even supported by -- the subscription series. Adding three more is
considered a high priority. Even an elongated preview period like the
Goodman's can sell out on subscription when the theatre offers a deeper
discount and/or other incentives (post-show talks with actors and other
members of the production team, for instance), making it reasonably
lucrative to extend the number of previews. In New York City, Lincoln
Center Theatre schedules previews according to the demands of each show,
regularly offering as many as four weeks of previews. Some theatres have
experimented with longer rehearsal and preview periods by budgeting for
special schedules on one or two productions a year, even within a
traditional subscription series. Asked how many previews they need,
artistic directors usually answered that two weeks or more were necessary;
ideally, they said, it would depend on the needs of a specific project.

One of the ironies of this discussion is that the need for preview
time has stimulated among artistic directors a nostalgia for one of the
practices of the commercial theatre. When Broadway was thriving,
productions would sometimes spend many months out of New York, performing
before paying audiences across the country. The importance of this
period can be seen in these older commercial practices, where the rule of
thumb for a play in out-of-town tryouts was that rehearsal time with an
audience -- previews -- would at least equal the time spent without one.
"Tryouts" allowed months of rehearsal, revision and testing in a full-
scale, income-producing, performance environment. While the nonprofit
theatre has generally inherited the standard rehearsal format from the
commercial theatre, it has by and large not received the added benefits
of the tryout period, a situation that has not only limited time to make
significant changes in performance, but also created false and dangerous
expectations: that plays only need this short period of rehearsal to get
"finished" and that all plays need the same amount of time to rehearse.
In reality, most productions and most plays rarely get finished in so
short a period of time. Furthermore, the demands of each project are
unique; some plays only need three-and-a-half weeks of preparation, while
others, notably large-cast plays, plays undergoing rewrites and major
classics, could benefit from many weeks -- or even months -- of rehearsal
and sometimes years of advance planning.

Theatres in some communities have encountered strong resistance from
the press to longer preview periods, as well as to unscheduled addition
of previews and postponement of opening nights. In many cities critics
feel that after five or six previews a show's opening ceases to be

13

newsworthy, since many people have already seen it. Other critics have
refused requests from theatres to move their review date, a conflict that
has in some cases meant failure for productions that might have, with a
little extra time for important changes and less deadline pressure, done
quite well. Artistic directors wish out loud for a corps of theatre
reviewers more sensitive to the process and needs of the art. "How can
we educate the press about what we do?" more than one artistic director
has asked. The Alley Theatre (Houston) addressed the question by helping
obtain a travel grant for a local critic to see the work of other
theatres in the U.S. and abroad. One artistic director suggested that
theatres urge trustees and subscribers to write letters encouraging arts
editors to rearrange the priorities of reviewing. Theatres want
feedback, artistic directors insist. In fact, theatres in cities with
only one paper and one critic often feel cheated out of a larger critical
dialogue. Artistic directors want, however, to nurture the kind of
feedback that goes beyond "buyer's guide" reports; they want criticism
that educates audiences by putting particular works into larger contexts
and that takes the artistic process into account. "How can we create a
climate in which more serious criticism can take place?" they ask.

2. More flexibility needs to be built into rehearsal schedules, so
that the process is suited to the unique needs of the specific project.

One artistic director speaks for all: "Every project is unique.
Each needs a different way of working, a different process, a different
amount of time. But we try too hard to make the creative process
efficient. We go on as if each play can be shaped with the same cookie
cutter: three-and-a-half weeks of rehearsal, two techs, a handful of
dress rehearsals and previews, run and close. We're not making cookies.
We're bringing something new to life. That takes time."

Standing side-by-side as major themes in the TCG discussions among
artistic directors are the need to treat projects individually, as their
unique needs demand, and the need for more time. Are theatres trying to
do too much, many artistic directors wonder? Are there simply too many
productions to allow for necessary (and flexible) time in between? Work
time. Research time. Reflection and gestation time. How, they ask, can
we free up the necessary hours in the day, weeks in a year, years in a
career, to do the quality of work we're capable of -- to mount truly
personal and unique productions? Some theatres rehearse for as little as
two-and-a-half weeks, although approximately four weeks is the norm. As
a result, there is strong consensus among them that the rehearsal period
contains little or no time for exploration of possible interpretations
within a text, work with specific stylistic or language requirements,
research of the play's period or milieu and adjustment to the additional
demands of large-cast or longer plays. Despite the differences between
projects, The Tempest and The Gin Game are often allotted the same amount
of preparation time. Although theatres have some control over rehearsal
periods -- they can get more time if they pay for it -- it is often the
plays that most need it that can least afford the extra time. A large-

cast Shakespeare play, for example, automatically adds costs for actors' salaries and numbers of period costumes, making the prospect of buying more rehearsal time onerous.

One creative solution to the lack of rehearsal time has already been effectively used at South Coast Repertory (Costa Mesa, California). SCR budgets at the start of each season for two-and-a-half "swing" weeks of rehearsal. These additional weeks can be applied to any show needing extra time, as the need arises. Other theatres have created additional rehearsal weeks less formally by juggling the needs of an entire season, though the effort of such juggling can become a burden. "Everything I do has to be jerry-built," explained one artistic director. "There's nothing that seems permanent. I'm always grabbing a few weeks from one thing for another, so that we get what we need." One example he gave of this jerry-building was bringing in a show from another regional theatre in order to free up rehearsal weeks for one of the theatre's own productions.

The idea of co-productions or regional tours in which plays are mounted jointly by theatres or one theatre's production is presented at other theatres is being explored by many artistic directors for various reasons, which will be discussed throughout this paper. One advantage of these undertakings is that they buy rehearsal time. A play performing in three different theatres can benefit from three whole rehearsal periods. The additional weeks of preparation can be concentrated up front or spread out in between the runs at the different theatres, allowing a greater-than-usual level of exploration and completion.

A group of Upstate New York theatres has shared three productions over three years to enable them to do work on a larger scale. Some of these theatres are now considering co-productions specifically to gain rehearsal time. Another option under these circumstances is pooling rehearsal time -- using less than the double or triple hours allowed -- and applying the time saved to longer rehearsal periods on other plays. Likewise, presenting work already mounted elsewhere can buy rehearsal time for a theatre's own productions by assigning weeks not needed by the co-production to another production.

Another aspect of the desire to build more space into the rehearsal process involves rehearsing shorter days. Almost every artistic director asked favored five-hour days spread out over more weeks. They feel that the eight-hour rehearsal is too long to sustain the necessary energy of the process, and that the best work is done in the first five hours. (Actors participating in independent artist discussions agreed.) Also, they need more time to do their homework; the long day cuts into time actors and directors need outside rehearsal to go over the developments of the day and to prepare for the following day's work, as well as time needed for design meetings, research and private exploration. Furthermore, by shortening days, rehearsals would be interspersed with gestation periods, the spaces necessary for reflection and creative thought. Often what the artist needs, according to artistic directors, is the passage of calendar time, to advance their thinking and deepen their feeling about the work at hand. Repertory rehearsals, which spread the process out by alternating rehearsals of more than one project, allow for such time.

Technical and dress rehearsals are two stages of the process that artistic directors wish to extend. The brevity of most current schedules, artistic directors feel, prohibits any but the most minute changes in a show's physical production. There is never time to "go back to the drawing board," once all the pieces of the production puzzle are in place. The sets are built, the costumes fitted and finished, the lights are up and in place. Details remain to be changed, but not much more. Several participants cited as a more useful model the example of director Robert Wilson, who always asks for a workshop period during which he evolves and designs scenery, then goes away for as long as a year, coming back to rehearse again with complete tech. Wilson also has been known to have a mock-up of his sets built -- out of cardboard and pieces of stock scenery -- much as European opera houses do, so that he can see in rehearsal an approximation of the play audiences will see in performance. Some artistic directors believe that the regular presence of designers in earlier rehearsals would pay off in a similar way, creating a more organic relationship between the production as it evolves through rehearsal and the design. Ongoing involvement would also make more extensive revisions of design ideas possible because they could begin before the crunch of technical rehearsals. Nevertheless, artistic directors caution, their need to make more significant changes would necessitate both a different process of building a show and different production schedules from the ones to which theatre craftspeople are currently accustomed.

3. <u>Methods of scheduling and programming need to be more flexible in order to accommodate a variety of projects and developmental needs.</u>

One of the great successes in the nonprofit theatre movement over the past three decades has been the growth of programs designed to nurture playwrights and develop new plays. Without question, there are more playwrights working in the American theatre now than ever before. Some artistic directors speculate that the growth and decentralization of nonprofit theatre, together with a boom in activity devoted to new play development, have created more opportunities for playwrights. Increasingly, new play development has become the province of the nonprofit theatres. Work that used to be available only to Broadway producers is now being offered first to institutional theatres, partly because they have cultivated relationships with playwrights and partly because the costs of commercial theatre production make taking risks on new plays more difficult in that arena. Nonprofit theatres in America are now the source of most of the new play production in the country. In addition to work on the main stage, theatres have evolved subsidiary development programs. At this time, artistic directors feel ready to forge a conduit between this pool of work in development and the mainstream of the subscription season.

The idea of creating a "pipeline" of work in development was a concept often raised in the discussions to describe the kind of conduit artistic directors envision. The pool of work available to theatres might include anything they are working on, reading, negotiating for, workshopping, commissioning or planning to bring in from elsewhere. Ideally, this developmental stream of work would feed projects into later seasons as they became ready for full production, without having to adhere to the impracticality of announcement deadlines six months to a year in advance. The desire to feed work into the season as it is ready obviously runs counter to some of the demands of selling the subscription series outlined above.

Circle Repertory Company (New York) maintains an ongoing laboratory, where writers, directors and actors workshop projects over a period of years. Once ready and only then, many of these projects find their way into the mainstage season. The Wilma Theater forms part of its season in much the same way, with projects going through approximately four stages of development and then becoming part of the season when the artistic directors are convinced that they are ready.

Many theatres operate a less formal pipeline, fed by their relationships with outside artists. For example, rather than picking plays and then hiring artists to direct and design them, a few artistic directors have focused on hiring people they respect and admire who have projects in mind. The artistic director, in this case, would ask a director, designer, writer or actor what he or she most wants to work on, then enter into preliminary planning meetings, and, if the project seems to fit the needs of both the theatre and the individual artist, put it into the pipeline for early development or plug it into the season. Some theatres, like La Jolla Playhouse (California) and McCarter Theatre Company (Princeton, N.J.) almost exclusively rely on this method of selecting a season.

Similarly, many artistic directors feel that doing the best work on a play depends on having the best possible (not just the best available) cast. Currently, much casting happens just prior to the beginning of rehearsals, so that actors tend to be slotted in, much as plays are slotted into a season. Instead of asking, "Who is available next month to play King Lear?" as artistic directors are often forced to do, they would prefer to develop projects with such questions as: "Who in the country is ready to play Lear? Whom do we want to build a production of Streetcar around?" Once the questions were answered, the difficult job of scheduling and planning the project would begin, so that productions would grow out of the casting, instead of the other way around.

Many artistic directors have also expressed the desire to pursue projects initiated by designers, who rarely see themselves as catalysts for artistic projects. It is widely held that designers are, on the whole, among the theatre's most accomplished artists, and that, as a group, they represent an unusually consistent -- and high -- degree of craft. The heads of the institutional theatres are looking for ways to

involve them more collaboratively in the planning stages of seasons and
to build productions around design concepts rather than always around
directorial choices.

Some of the most exciting thought in theatres today focuses on the
creation of workshop and developmental programs separate from mainstage
seasons to counter what artists see as an increased result-orientation in
a theatre that grew up as an alternative to the product-centered
commercial theatre. "Our theatres were formed, in large part, for
research and development," one artistic director explained. "That's what
we did. That was our main function. Now research and development is
subordinate to what we do, and we're so busy trying to survive that we
feel we have to tie our developmental programs into our main product."

A healthy research and development program, artistic directors
agree, is essential to theatre art and needs to be economically sustained
in and of itself, for itself, not bounded by other constrictions.
Workshop programs are intended to re-emphasize research and development
as the foundation of the nonprofit theatre. Eureka Theatre Company in
San Francisco, for instance, has established a new play development fund,
based on the belief that it takes three years to develop a play. The
projects begin with the idea for the play; as a political theatre Eureka
is particularly interested in content. A three-year plan is then
developed by the playwright and the theatre's dramaturg, in order to find
the ideal process -- that is, the one that works best for each individual
project. Upon completion of a rough draft, a variety of workshops are
possible, all involving actors, a director and designers. Some theatres
are channeling their resources into commissioning programs. South Coast
Repertory (Costa Mesa, Calif.) has an unusually extensive commissioning
program, where substantial commissions for five writers are a line item
in the annual budget. While these commissions sometimes result in plays
for South Coast's season, there is no guarantee that they will; the
commission program guarantees only an investment in the writer, and a
commitment to research and development for the stage.

The value of such programs is that they support artists, rather than
merely buying plays. Goodman Theatre (Chicago) has channeled the
proceeds of an extended run of a successful musical directly into a
"creative development" fund, e.g. commissioning. Since this income had
not been budgeted, the artistic director, the managing director and the
board believed it was appropriate to apply the funds, derived from an
artistic success, back into the development of future artistic programs.
One such program was the instigation of a potential collaboration between
two successful playwrights, where commission money was advanced just to
allow them to sit down together and explore the idea of collaborating.
Once they settled on an idea for the collaboration, the second stage of
the commission -- early draft writing -- began, with additional funds
advanced by the theatre.

Some theatres with an interest in commissioning and long-term
development, even those with the money to do so, face the limitations of
their staffing when they try to follow through on the commissions; there

must be someone on staff free to see through the progress of long-range work, to work with the playwright, arrange meetings between the artists involved and provide support as needed in an ongoing way. Again, time is the crucial issue, especially as the artistic staffs of most theatres are so small to begin with. Research and development, essential to the creation of a body of work, as opposed to merely picking seasons, is the area that cries out for artistic associates, literary staffs and artistic directors free enough to concentrate on developing the work that comprises the theatre's artistic life.

Co-productions and second productions can also function as a form of development. Because a production can be worked on over a period of time, the production -- not simply the play -- can be developed and advanced. Designs can be altered, performances deepened, staging improved, and the whole project more completely explored and finished. This type of process emphasizes the truth that first and second productions are, at best, drafts for better productions, and that the work is never "done." Co-productions invest in the ongoing life of projects, the working out of a director's vision of a production over time and the maturation of performances. When a second production is planned, more work can be done during a show's run, the process being continuous. Unfortunately, co-productions are too often viewed in financial terms as a way of saving money, rather than as a process of deepening and perfecting art, a process which may end up costing just as much as separate productions. Moreover, longer periods of work allow time for gestation between productions. Speaking of a second run of the original company of Marsha Norman's 'night Mother at the Mark Taper Forum a good time after the show's first Los Angeles and Broadway runs, Gordon Davidson, the Taper's artistic director marvelled, "The depth and brilliance of the company's work together the second time around was something that no amount of rehearsal could have given them. By the time they were together again, it was as if they had lived those lives."

As in the work of any laboratory, there is a great deal of theatrical research and development that will never, should never see the light of performance. Because this work costs time and money, and because it runs the risk of never producing income, it is often among the first cuts in budgeting and planning. Nevertheless, the value of development in the care and feeding of the life of a theatre can't be underestimated. Artistic directors continue to look for ways to do and support this vital work. McCarter Theatre, for instance, has instituted a series of workshops separate from the work of the season. After raising money for a specific workshop and hiring a company to participate, these artists spend three or four weeks away from the theatre, working on a specific artistic problem, which could be anything from improvisations based on a novel to the exploration of storytelling techniques, work that may or may not find their way into later seasons.

Another way artistic directors are exploring to add flexibility to their current methods of programming seasons involves collaboration with other artistic directors at the season planning stages. As a response to their own isolation, artistic directors suggested planning seasons, or at least brainstorming about creative possibilities for seasons, at retreats with other artistic directors. Some also utilize planning committees of artistic directors and associate artists (associate artistic directors, literary managers, playwrights, designers, directors and actors). At least one artistic director brings in other leading artists as consultants to help discuss plays and select seasons, thereby cutting down on artistic isolation and stimulating the creative thought needed to find new flexibility in the institutional structures that can sometimes seem unyielding.

THINKING BEYOND FOUR WALLS:

THE INDIVIDUAL ARTIST AS A NATIONAL PRIORITY

"Our first responsibility is to the artist: to protect
the artist and to allow the artist's whisper to become
a voice."

> -- Richard Hopkins
> Artistic Director
> Florida Studio Theatre

"Theatre is at its best when it speaks to the human
spirit. We need more of that spiritual presence on
our staffs."

> -- John Dillon
> Artistic Director
> Milwaukee Repertory Theater

The single most pressing concern for the majority of artistic
directors across the nation is to find ways of keeping the most talented
artists in the theatre. A clear pattern of artists moving away from
theatre, they argue, has already begun. As work in television and film
continues to offer extraordinary compensation and celebrity (with its
attendant artistic independence) that is unavailable in a decentralized
theatre, and as generations of new artists raised with the allure of
media before them enter the arena, the need to strengthen the attractions
of the theatre as a profession intensifies. Moreover, for the
profession's mature artists -- actors, writers, directors and designers
-- who have grown up along with the nonprofit theatre in America, the
theatre must find a way to accommodate their changing needs and to
celebrate their experience and achievement. Failing to do so, artistic
directors anticipate, the theatre will lose them to more lucrative
fields.

Described in this way, the situation may sound dire; indeed, the
majority of artistic directors believe it is. Moreover, they see the
nurturing of artists as a national issue which must be addressed by the
entire theatre community working together. Certainly, individual theatres
can help create conditions which attract artists to the theatre.
Artistic directors agree that the commitment each theatre makes to
artists affects other theatres, the profession and the art form as a
whole. Nevertheless, the problem is too widespread, they feel, for any
one theatre to solve. Most artistic directors share an awareness that
continuing media dominance and a growing stress on financial advancement
are cultural and societal trends beyond the control of individuals or
single institutions. They are eager to find cooperative means of

counteracting the effect of this changing climate within the theatre.

Artistic directors involved in the TCG meetings asked probing questions of themselves in order to understand their own responsibility for what they perceive to be a reduced commitment by artists toward the theatre. "Are we still interesting to artists?" one group asked. "Are there too many theatres?" questioned another. "Have we made artists welcome enough in our theatres? Do we commit ourselves to their long-term development more than the media do, or do we, like television and film, offer only occasional employment to satisfy our needs, rather than considering the needs of the artists?" asked a third.

In addition to the self-examination this probing inspired, a striking feature of these discussions was their future orientation; artistic directors are concerned with the long-range growth of the artists and the art, and seem dedicated to finding creative ideas to insure the continued development of both. In this way, the institutional structure of nonprofit theatre differs from the single-project orientation of the media and the commercial theatre. It trades and invests in futures, even as it fights for survival day-to-day. A theatre that commissions a play has no guarantee of "product"; it has, instead, invested in the continuing development of a writer. Likewise, a theatre that employs actors fresh out of training programs is speculating on talent for the future of the theatre as a whole. More than its commercial kin, the nonprofit theatre must always balance the needs of the present with the unknowns of the future. This double focus appears everywhere in the discussion below, as artistic directors look to their own immediate requirements while watching over an uncertain time to come, as they work to preserve the unique identities of their own individual theatres while seeing to the guardianship of the profession and the art form.

1. <u>Artistic directors are concerned with keeping artists in the theatre; they need to constantly renew their commitment to making their theatres homes for artists.</u>

Although America's institutional theatres are the principal employers of thousands of artists and the number of theatres offering such employment has grown consistently over the past three decades, artistic directors still don't feel they have been able to do enough. In fact, according to artistic directors, not one category of theatre artist (actors, writers, directors or designers) has yet developed a truly satisfactory relationship to the institutional theatre. The improvement of these relationships depends on a complex of factors, including: working conditions, creative climate and opportunities, compensation, active involvement/participation in the theatre's ongoing life, as well as national and regional recognition and visibility, especially for mature artists.

"How can theatres make it possible for artists to stay in the profession?" the question goes. One common answer: "Pay them more." Certainly, adequate compensation is a goal too rarely achieved, even though attaining living wages for artists in the theatre has been a primary aim of the institutions since their inception. Still, compensation is only one part of the equation artistic directors consider when facing the potential drain of talent from the field. Reasons for staying in the theatre are as varied as those for getting into it in the first place. Many of these reasons, artistic directors believe, are human ones; the rewards of healthy collaborative exchange, artistic self-expression and a supportive environment for creativity stack up alongside financial rewards as priorities. Many artists are drawn to the theatre for these very rewards, and all need them for sustenance. One artistic director argued persuasively that his theatre had lost track of these human needs, giving priority to financial and programmatic resources over human ones. "We've been coming at it the wrong way," he explained to his board. "The order needs to be reversed." This train of thought led to a total and drastic restructuring of a large institutional theatre, one that involved cuts, program changes, different hiring priorities and a better way of making theatre.

The artists at the heart of the theatre have individual needs; they require individual treatment. Their inspiration springs from a range of sources, their working methods vary and their lives place different demands on them. In most cases, their process even changes from project to project, depending on the material, their preparation, their collaborators and their growth as artists. All of them, though, artistic directors insist, need to feel more at home in the theatre, less like "jobbers," hired hands brought in to fulfill a function and then move on. They need, instead, a greater involvement in the ongoing life of the individual theatre and the community of artists, administrators and audience who fuel that life.

Some of the ways artistic directors have explored of making artists feel more at home in the theatres entail simple gestures aimed at improving working conditions and involving artists. One artistic director told the story of a major playwright who, having been supplied with business cards by a theatre producing his work, went away in great excitement, showing off the cards, on which his name and his affiliation to the theatre were embossed. In more than two decades of writing for the theatre, he had never had his own card; this small gift gave him a stronger sense of belonging, of having a stake in that theatre. In meetings of independent artists which supplemented the artistic director discussions, other playwrights expressed the need for work space, during periods of residency at theatres. No matter how long their stay, they need some quiet, private space to think and rewrite. Artistic directors believe that responding to this simple request by making a desk, typewriter and quiet, private space available is something which can and should be done.

The need for adequate housing is another space issue affecting the working conditions of guest artists. Many artistic directors feel passionately that decent living conditions for visiting actors, directors, designers and writers must be a priority. For artists working away from home, they argue, a pleasant place to live when provided by the theatre (as opposed to a housing allowance for the artists to find their own rooms) can diminish the feeling of impermanance, thereby making the artist feel cared for -- less like a casual employee. Quite a few theatres with the resources and a commitment to better living quarters for guest artists have bought apartments or buildings for housing, finding the investment more beneficial in the long run than renting on an ongoing basis. At one meeting, artistic directors swapped unsettling stories about reactions to suitable housing: a senior actress was surprised that the younger actors were given housing without a contract fight; a grateful actor was worried about "deserving" the good treatment he received. The artistic directors expressed concern over these stories, concern that artists have had too few truly good experiences and, so, don't expect enough from the theatres. Again, many believe that the treatment an artist receives at one theatre affects his or her commitment to theatre in general.

Small efforts on the part of a theatre to treat artists well can make a big difference. Comfortably furnished guest rooms with access to personal phones, working televisions and usable office equipment -- even fresh flowers -- create an atmosphere more conducive to creative work. By arranging transportation, such as rides to local stores and restaurants or car pools for days off, theatres can put artists at ease in cities strange to them. The Alley Theatre provides actors with cars, a necessity in a place the size of Houston. One artistic director said he meets every arriving actor at the train, thereby making that actor feel welcome and important. Some theatres provide meals for actors between matinees and evening performances, even when not contracted to do so. Often these meals are arranged by volunteer hospitality groups who plan parties and other functions to help guest artists feel at home. Many theatres have successfully mobilized volunteers to come up with their own welcoming methods.

Because the treatment artists receive at a theatre so strongly influences their career choices, one artistic director maintained that the company manager is among the key positions on any staff. Someone must be found for this job who understands the needs of actors and attends to those needs.

Individual artists, like artistic directors, draw inspiration from many sources and, therefore, require time and space for thought, reflection and work. Some artists function well with deadlines; as one artistic director put it, "Alot of us are adrenaline freaks." Others need longer periods of privacy, pressureless workshops and continued support from artistic staff. Some artists are demanding; others easy-going. Occasionally artistic directors warned against hiring the easy over the demanding without reference to their talent, cautioning that collaborating with people who "don't make waves" doesn't ensure better art. Again, the key word was "flexibility," with artistic directors looking for ways to accommodate different working styles, processes and temperaments.

Flexible scheduling is an issue for individual artists, too. For mostly economic reasons, independent artists tend to schedule jobs back-to-back, in order to do as much work over the course of a year as possible. Often, it is hard to squeeze in even necessary time for planning, rumination and for the completion of thinking about projects. A director, for instance, having opened one show, might already be preparing a next one, and may even be starting into rehearsals immediately. That director's work would benefit from time between productions or time at the first theatre once the show had opened, to reflect on the experience. This opportunity for reflection could enrich the director's next project and develop for the profession more self-aware directors, able to use the lessons of each project in the preparation of future work. Artistic directors and independent artists alike are frustrated with a system that makes working on a production after it has opened almost impossible; everyone has to move on to the next in the lineup. This rigidity reinforces the "product" mentality artistic directors are determined to break out of. More time can be contracted or built into the process, they believe, if the commitment is there.

Likewise, many artistic directors wish to create more time up front for planning future projects. They wish, for example, to be able to involve designers in the early, conceptual stages of planning, often as much as a year before rehearsals begin. This advance work would allow them to utilize the expertise of the designer in the director's early thinking and, perhaps, in some of the later stages of the playwright's revision (when working on new plays). More time for planning and completion is necessary, artistic directors believe, if theatres wish to better challenge theatre artists and ensure their most creative work.

Creative collaborations excite artists. The rewards of such collaborations cannot be overestimated, artistic directors agree. A good way to keep artists in the theatre, they say, is to surround them with other, equally interesting artists. The theatres reap substantial rewards as well, for, as one artistic director explained, "The best work happens when strong artists work with other strong artists in supported situations." Nurturing these partnerships may involve theatres keeping teams of collaborators together or creating new collaborations among major artists. It may involve asking artists whom they want to work with. Directors have their favorite designers, designers often work best with colleagues they've worked with before and actors are usually an excellent source of information about other talented actors. In any case, fostering exciting collaborations is part of the renewed commitment artistic directors desire to create the kind of home where groups of mature artists feel they can do their best work together.

2. Theatres and artists alike need to find creative ways to address the chronic undercompensation in the field.

Clearly, keeping artists in the theatre is a nationwide priority, requiring a commitment from all theatres. While artistic directors believe that this commitment can be demonstrated through the creation of more welcoming and exciting working conditions, they also are deeply concerned with the broad issues of compensation. On the most fundamental of those issues, artistic directors are unanimous: nonprofit theatres don't yet pay artists enough; they still don't pay them what their training or experience merits. Artistic directors were candid and outspoken on this score. "I have no answer for actors who tell me they're tired of subsidizing regional theatre," one said. Artistic directors are also unanimous about wanting to be able to pay artists more. In fact, a major reason for founding many institutional theatres was to create places where artists could work consistently and earn a living wage.

Each theatre has its own aesthetic priorities and will allocate its finite resources according to its own lights. Naturally, the theatre that provides a laboratory for writers advocates most strongly for increased financial support to playwrights; the theatre whose work is rooted in sustaining an acting ensemble suffers more deeply from conditions which keep actors from making seasonal commitments. The same partisanship holds for theatres stressing production and design, directorial ingenuity or acting power. Indeed, in a theatre community which thrives on individual vision and uniqueness, there is no need for consensus about who is the most important artist in the theatre. There is, however, consensus that every group of artists in the theatre profession is an endangered species in need of increased economic support and protection if the institutional theatres are to maintain a vital connection to the heart of their enterprise -- the individual artist. [*]

----

[*]

The expression of concern from artistic directors in national meetings was passionately underscored by independent artists in a separate series of meetings across the country, sponsored by TCG. At these discussions leading playwrights, designers, directors and actors expressed deep frustration at not being able to make a living or maintain a life while doing the work they love in the theatre. The pull to work outside of the theatre has, they say, become stronger and more urgent. This is especially true of more experienced artists who, having worked in the field for 10 to 20 years (sometimes longer), have new sets of demands -- such as, educating their children. Many have come to believe that theatre is a young person's profession, with no place for people over 40. These artists have witnessed the rapid growth of the institutions at the same time their own earning power seems to have leveled off. Their sense of alienation and disenfranchisement is profound, yet in most cases their love of theatre remains unabated. These meetings more than confirmed artistic directors' fears: the theatre is in danger of losing its artists.

The most visible siphoning off of talent from the theatre is the draw of stage actors to the media. Stories of weekly salaries in film and TV topping the yearly earnings of regularly employed theatre actors are commonplace. No artistic director in America begrudges actors those fees or blames them for wanting to work in the media. While artistic directors admit that the theatres haven't realized perfect situations for artists, they are troubled by what they see as a growing difficulty of getting and keeping commitments from actors. The possibility of other, more lucrative work, they say, has made actors hesitant to commit to theatre work in advance. Similarly, they find it hard to get extended commitments (season-length, for example) from actors -- who fear the loss of commercial work. Moreover, they are distressed that some actors fail to honor commitments once they have been made.

Artistic directors know that stage skills atrophy without practice; they argue that actors who work away from the theatre for too long without "flexing their muscles" and confronting a live audience can lose the technique necessary to sustain a performance. They also know that, while it is now possible for actors to earn a modest living working fulltime in the nonprofit theatre, it is not possible for theatres to compete nor expect ever to compete with the media.

Realizing that the salaries they pay individual artists must often support their families as well, artistic directors asked themselves and each other what kind of yearly salary might be considered respectable enough to keep actors working in the theatre. The question of such a goal for at least medium to larger-sized institutional theatres came up frequently at the meetings. Their hypothetical estimates varied, though many suggest that a mid-career actor employed year-round should reasonably be able to expect to earn a salary commensurate with those offered faculty members in academic institutions (ranging from $33,000 a year for assistant professors to $52,000 for full professors, according to the U.S. Department of Education).

In America's decentralized theatre, geography also plays a part in the career decisions actors make. It has become increasingly difficult to find actors willing to leave commercial production centers, like New York, Los Angeles and Chicago even for short periods of time. Even the most reputable and successful theatres outside these cities, including those paying some of the highest salaries, have trouble attracting actors from the three centers for major roles. To combat this problem when planning its repertory series of new plays, Baltimore's Center Stage made sure to schedule it after the television pilot season, in hopes that fewer actors would resist an extended stay in Maryland. The general unavailability is as true of young actors as it is of more experienced ones, whose schedules are virtually impossible to work around, artistic directors say. The film and TV industries are looking for younger and younger talent, and many training programs are focusing less on developing actors for the theatre than on cultivating the media potential in their students. Even those recent graduates who don't have job offers and signs of promise for careers in media are, according to artistic directors, loathe to leave the cities where commercial possibilities exist. A major midwestern theatre had to consider dozens of young ingenues before it could find one who would even read for a lead role that represented six months of work. The situation is most grave for theatres seeking mature, male character actors. In addition, nearly all artistic directors have lost actors to television and film opportunities in the days or hours immediately preceding first rehearsals or even once rehearsals and/or performances had begun. The tenuousness of these commitments has rendered futile attempts to plan productions around given actors far in advance, prompting one artistic director to exclaim, "We're better off casting the morning of first rehearsal than nine months ahead!"

While the gravity of this situation seems to have increased in recent years, artistic directors are at a loss for a remedy. As a group they are torn between the desire to see actors take advantage of these lucrative opportunities and the impulse to be more forceful in demanding that contracts and commitments be honored. Most feel that any action taken in isolation is weak. For example, if one theatre lets an actor out of a commitment and another tries to hold an actor to a contract, then, artistic directors feel, the theatre community is sending out mixed messages. Many artistic directors are concerned that the apparent ease with which commitments in theatre are broken is symptomatic of trends in society as a whole, where financial gain is the prime measure of success and where the cultural influence of an under-subsidized theatre has diminished.

Most important, artistic directors blame themselves for complicity in this dynamic; they don't always demonstrate a strong enough commitment to the actor, they argue, to make the actor want to commit to them. Artistic directors are exploring ways of deepening their own commitment to actors and providing more security for them. Demonstrating a willingness to create long-term work for actors is one way artistic directors are exploring of strengthening their relationships with actors; they know, however, that the difficulty of finding actors for short-term projects is compounded when theatres are looking for seasonal commitments, especially in regions lacking opportunities for outside commercial work.

Some artistic directors believe that the disintegration of the acting ensemble in American theatre since the '60s and '70s has reinforced the feeling of insecurity within the acting community, thrown actors back on their own resources and made it necessary for them to pursue the most lucrative work available just to survive during inevitable stretches of unemployment. These artistic directors believe that the promise of 40 weeks' work would make actors feel more secure, more willing to choose theatre as a fulltime profession. Seattle Repertory Theatre and Berkeley Repertory Theatre have recently established small core resident companies in cities which have talent pools but limited opportunities, but where artists choose to live. There is, however, little optimism that this situation will improve nationally. Even the best minds in the American theatre working together seem able to find only partial solutions, though they agree that attempts must continue.[*]

Although a growing number of artistic directors are attracted to the goal of creating resident companies, most agree that the current economics of theatre -- a shrinking funding community and expanding theatre community, the pull of the film and TV industries, increased real estate costs and so on -- conspire against permanent ensembles. One artistic director, for instance, explained that six members of his 10-person ensemble made over $100,000 each from film work last year; "I won't be able to keep them here now," he explained. Another artistic director complained that the difficulty of casting in the current environment-- with casting directors and agents mediating between the theatre and the artist, and with a new complexity in scheduling resulting from actors crossing over between media -- has taken up so much of his time that he would consider casting entirely from a resident company in order to free up the theatre's (and his) time.

Conceivably, the ensemble of the '90s would little resemble the ensemble of the '60s and '70s. Some artistic directors envision larger, looser networks of actors that can be retained and salaried year-round (perhaps by more than one institution) and shared among groups of theatres or within theatre communities. This type of association has already begun to happen in an informal way. The theatres in Seattle, for instance, have all shared actors and so provided them with work varied

----

*

As one alternative solution, a number of theatres actively seek outside work for actors whenever possible, to supplement their salaries and connect them more strongly with the community. Such efforts are intended to demonstrate a commitment to the actors by accommodating the economic realities of their profession. Remains Theatre (Chicago), for example, maintains an acting ensemble in a city with numerous film and TV opportunities. By helping actors find media work, this small theatre can support their needs for more money and greater visibility, while enabling them to keep working at the theatre. Even though Capital Rep (Albany, N.Y.) relies on visiting artists, the theatre's artistic directors help guest actors find supplemental voice-over and commercial work to open up the kinds of employment opportunities that might inspire them to return to work in Albany. The Guthrie Theater (Minneapolis) encouraged the actors to organize a talent agency to capitalize on the radio and television work provided by advertising agencies in the city. Other theatres, like American Repertory Theatre (Cambridge, Mass.) and American Conservatory Theatre (San Francisco), arrange teaching opportunities as sources of additional income for their actors. The Oregon Shakespearean Festival offers docent tours of the facility, led by actors, who earn extra money as guides.

and constant enough to keep them in the community. Chicago has a strong community of actors and ensemble groups that remain fairly fluid, working regularly throughout the community and in media. American Conservatory Theatre (San Francisco), which has maintained a resident company throughout its 22-year history, now has a large pool of alumni who share a common vocabulary and create an informal, extended company. Artistic directors also discussed co-productions between theatres as a method of sharing actors, providing longer employment and giving actors exposure to a larger, more diverse audience.

This exposure can be important to actors who already feel that stage work limits their potential visibility. As previously discussed, the celebrity possible from performing in a decentralized theatre can't compete with the popular recognition film and television make possible. Artistic directors believe that theatres can improve this situation by concerted efforts to move actors and productions around, and from consistent press initiatives to celebrate theatre actors. One artistic director suggested dubbing a whole year "the year of the actor."

Like actors, designers and directors feel the pull from film and television, and, while their exodus is less pronounced, it is equally devastating. Because they are engaged by theatres on a similar basis, they share similar problems. Many leading stage directors have already turned to directing soap operas for a more substantial income, for example, while the music video industry has become an exciting outlet for designers' talents. Artistic directors particularly fear the loss of the theatre's mature and experienced artists. In part, the process of re-evaluation described in this report was prompted by the effects of a "middle-age crisis" in the American theatre. Institutions which have survived through the first bursts of growth in the '60s and '70s and achieved some stability during their adolescent years have reached a plateau in their development requiring them to look simultaneously backward to the lessons and achievements of the past, and forward to the undiscovered territory of the future. Meanwhile, the rise of second and even third-generation theatres within the nonprofit movement have continued to alter the landscape of the profession. Similarly, independent artists in the theatre have grown up along with one generation or another of theatres, and those who have reached the top of the profession see themselves, according to artistic directors, repeating the past with no sense of where to grow from here, either financially or artistically.

As a profession, the theatre has never developed a system for honoring or compensating its senior artists who remain independent of a particular institution. In the words of one artistic director, "We pay too little to keep the artists we most revere." While individual theatres might pay certain designers more than others, for example, there exists no profession-wide standard for recognizing experience, achievement or continued service. The theatre provides no sufficient incentives for mature artists to stay in the field, no opportunities for promotion or advancement, few rewards for distinction. In part, artistic directors' concerns stem from an awareness that the theatrical professions in America aren't structured as they are in other countries. We don't operate a graduated system of proficiency in the crafts: from apprentice to journeyman to associate, senior and distinguished artist, for instance. The lack of such steps can make careers seem static. American Repertory Theatre (Cambridge, Mass.) is attempting to create this kind of system, asking company artists to consider their relationships a 10-year commitment and creating distinctions between levels of experience. This system is modeled on ballet companies, in which an artist establishes a whole career in association with a single company, advancing from the school to the corps before becoming a principal dancer and senior company member.

Admittedly, artistic directors want to work in two directions at once: they want to encourage young talent without artificial distinctions of proficiency, while, at the same time, finding ways of keeping senior artists supported and growing. Artistic directors also feel they don't invest enough time or energy in locating and hiring young directors. Nor do they take the steps necessary to infiltrate training programs as a way of identifying young talents, whom they could encourage and support through the early stages of their careers. Because of its teaching function as part of the university, Yale Repertory Theatre is perhaps unique in its use of young directors; some of Yale's third-year graduate students are able to direct shows at the Rep, while the design students have the experience of designing for Rep productions, and student actors are cast in the shows. Center Stage (Baltimore) retains a director as Associate Artist, who, in addition to her own directing work, is responsible for scouting young talent and seeing work outside of Baltimore which the artistic director may be unable to see. Other artistic directors reinforced the value of artistic directors continuing to meet and talk among themselves, thus using each other as resources for identifying interesting directors.

One problem artistic directors say all freelance directors and designers share is that they must do too many projects a year to earn even a meager living. Directors can expect a reasonable income only by working on seven or eight projects a year. Artistic directors agree, though, that directors wishing to do their best work should direct no more than, say, four plays in a year. Too many directors, tired of the constant grind for so little reward and looking for stability, become artistic directors; as a result, the wrong people may take on a job that demands very different skills. Similarly, designers are forced to cram an unreasonable number of projects into a season just to survive. This nearly impossible undertaking squeezes out time for advance planning, as well as the ability for designers to remain in residence during a significant portion of the rehearsal process. Costume designers, whose work keeps them in the theatres longer, have even more severe limitations on their time. Again, this overload becomes harder as artists get older and their personal obligations expand, along with the desire to stop the grind and explore less work more deeply.

Like the flow of actors away from live theatre, the difficulty of keeping and supporting the careers of designers and directors is a national problem requiring broad and cooperative solutions. One approach suggested by artistic directors would draw on the pooled resources of several theatres. For instance, a group of individual theatres might commit to an artist for a season, thereby insuring a secure living and recognizing publicly that the caliber of this artist's work is worthy of collective support. In this way Los Angeles Theatre Center, Mark Taper Forum (Los Angeles), Old Globe Theatre (San Diego) and South Coast Repertory (Costa Mesa) are considering committing to the work of a single director for a season, with the promise of a livable salary and a directing assignment in each of the four theatres. The artistic director of one of the nation's largest nonprofit theatres voiced strong support for the current relationship between theatres of varying size, a kind of big brotherhood among theatres where larger institutions take the responsibility for paying artists more, in order to make it possible for them to also accept work in smaller theatres with fewer financial resources. Other artistic directors recommended that the theatres take a more active role in finding flexible university teaching positions for top designers in their own regions as a way of asserting their commitment to getting more money for theatre professionals, and investing in future talent as well.

Artistic directors are equally concerned about the complex arrangements between theatres and playwrights. Now that new plays are done almost exclusively in nonprofit theatres, they feel the need to evaluate their methods of compensating playwrights. American playwrights, too, are drawn away from theatre by the media, as both film and TV have begun to tap their talents. Writers work and earn in wholly different ways from other theatre artists; they may spend years on a play before they make any money from its production, although their work has more potential for continuing earnings than does that of other theatre artists. Rarely are they compensated for their time -- time writing or time in residence at a theatre -- as are other artists in work-for-hire situations; rather, they are paid for certain rights to their "properties," an arrangement involving issues of ownership of the work. Some artistic directors believe that rethinking current methods of compensating writers -- perhaps toward a combination of fees for their time, royalties for the production of their "properties" and commissions for future work -- is necessary.

Some artistic directors feel that the current system of paying writers royalties for productions in nonprofit theatres, which the nonprofits borrowed from the commercial theatre practice, is inappropriate in this arena because, being dependent on ticket sales, it is the only area of artistic compensation that is tied to the financial success or failure of the project, even though the playwright's effort is the same either way. While at larger institutional theatres, playwrights stand a chance of making a significant income from royalties, productions at smaller theatres with lower potential earnings can be financially riskier for writers. More than one artistic director suggested that smaller theatres and theatres doing workshops of a play might pay fees to writers, guaranteeing them a specific wage, even if larger theatres stick to royalty arrangements in order to avoid imposing a ceiling on earnings.

A number of suggestions arose for increasing compensation to playwrights through alternative means. The payment of an additional fee or salary to a writer for attending rehearsals or advising a theatre on a second production of a play was one such idea proposed. The National Theatre of Great Britain employs this system as a way of compensating playwrights for their time, as well as for their plays. Playwrights-on-payroll programs, playwright residencies and associate artistic director or dramaturg positions for playwrights were also cited. Another proposal involves a collective action among a group of theatres to support a single playwright for a set time period. For example, a group of theatres interested in the work of the same writer might guarantee that writer a salary for a year, in addition to preparing one production each of any play authored by that person. The writer, therefore, would be getting a secure wage, fees or royalties from three productions and exposure for his or her work in three separate communities.

Because of the time writers spend working before they receive any compensation, parcelling out percentages of that play's future earnings is a sensitive issue, especially if those percentages cut into the writer's own share. Certainly no theatre sets out to curtail a writer's future earnings. Yet in spite of their rarity, the handful of nonprofit-developed works that became huge commercial successes and funneled large amounts of money back to the institutions unfortunately stand, as one artistic director put it, like beacons over all discussions of compensation to playwrights. Artistic directors are divided over how best to ensure higher earnings for playwrights, while protecting their own interests in the event of substantial commercial success. A few argue that new play production has become common enough to cut its risks and continue to take no share, preserving instead all future earnings for the playwright. Many others still see new work as a risky business which draws on the theatre's resources in a way that earns for the theatre a stake in or share of future profits.

A natural tension of interests therefore results from the potential of income generated by a successful commercial future life. Too often, artistic directors feel, this tension is further fomented by agents, operating as mediators between theatres and writers and, so, keeping them in separate corners instead of encouraging mutually beneficial arrangements. One frequent suggestion would guarantee playwrights a minimum income -- from subsequent productions -- before the original producer would take a percentage. Even in this case, artistic directors hope that this percentage could come out of the commercial producer's share rather than the writer's. When a subsequent nonprofit theatre wants to develop a play that has already premiered at another nonprofit theatre, it was also suggested that the two theatres involved in shaping the work might forge a shared arrangement to split the theatre share of future earnings without penalizing the playwright. South Coast Repertory (Costa Mesa, Calif.) has pared down the length of its involvement in the future life of plays developed there. SCR takes a percentage of the writer's share only in the event of a commercial production and only if that production occurs within two years of its own.

The level of commitment a theatre makes to the individual artist goes beyond questions of compensation or working conditions for a single project. The difference between paying a playwright a larger guarantee against royalties and supporting a writer's ongoing career or involving him or her in the daily life of the theatre is a significant one. Moreover, reintegrating independent artists into the fabric of the institutions can have an enormous impact on the American theatre as a whole, as well as on the art form. Consider as an example of commitment by the profession to individual artists the hypothetical question asked by one artistic director: "If every theatre in America adopted a playwright, what would be the impact five years down the road?" Obviously, the possible effect of such an action -- or any similar widespread adoption of artists -- would be remarkable. According to this artistic director, relations between the institutions and American writers could be revitalized, practically reinvented; a body of stageworthy new work, probably surpassing in size that of any similar period of time, might be available to audiences; the collective nature of the action could signal the country that the nonprofit theatre is alive, healthy and ready to lay groundwork for the future. Even a purely theoretical suggestion like this one demonstrates the incalculable potential effect of collective action by theatres. So extraordinary a measure would require a widespread commitment to forming relationships with artists that go far beyond "doing a show" and would give artists a stake in the ongoing lives of the institutions. While an action like this can't and shouldn't be legislated, it exemplifies the kind of active participation and complex effort (including more creative working conditions, recognition of senior artists and increased compensation to all) that artistic directors have been discussing for involving artists more completely in the theatre and keeping them there.

3. <u>Theatres need to build better long-term relationships with artists and find ways of integrating them into the ongoing life of the institutions.</u>

Across the country many artistic directors have already initiated programs intended to build stronger long-term relationships between artists and the theatres. The artistic directors are individually and as a group reexamining the possibility of maintaining resident companies of actors; creating residencies for writers, directors and designers; establishing staff positions for associate artistic directors; developing artistic associate programs; exploring ways of making guest artists feel more involved in the creative life of the institution; and cultivating loose affiliations and networks of artists.

34

Some of the difficulties of maintaining acting ensembles have already been discussed. The fact remains, however, that while there is no consensus on this point, many artistic directors long to develop companies in their theatres. These companies, they believe, would allow them to create a more coherent body of work, and a distinctive and consistent acting style, both of which serve as a defense against what one artistic director termed "schmearing into indistinctiveness." These artistic directors feel that resident acting companies enable theatres to rediscover themselves as laboratories for art by making a greater range of research and development programs possible and affordable. Working in a company, they say, stretches actors through the opportunities to act regularly in a variety of parts. Moreover, the presence of a company enriches a theatre by deepening its artistic resources, so that the theatre needn't rely solely on the voice of a single artist (the artistic director).

There are two types of permanent acting companies operating in America: resident ensembles performing in mainstream institutional theatres and smaller ensembles or collectives. For the most part, the collective ensembles have chosen to devote themselves to the development of a body of work reflecting a group aesthetic. Experimental companies begun in the '60s and early '70s like the Dell'Arte Players Company (Blue Lake, Calif.), Mabou Mines (New York City), the Roadside Theater (Whitesburg, KY), the San Francisco Mime Troupe, Theatre X (Milwaukee) and The Wooster Group (New York City) have opted for a kind of lifestyle and way of working over the possibility of financial success. The quality and longevity of the companies have demonstrated that ensembles can work if their repertoires are special. While geographical and size limitations may not affect these groups -- they build theatre around the number of actors in the ensemble -- sustaining an economically restrictive way of life becomes more difficult as company members get older and their needs change.

For mainstream theatres, geography is a critical factor influencing their ability to maintain resident acting companies. Many artistic directors agreed that trying to maintain year-round resident companies near New York and Los Angeles -- with the ever-present lure of other employment opportunities -- is essentially futile. At the same time, many feel that acting companies in regions remote from theatre centers like New York can provide a necessary security for actors. Unfortunately, it has become increasingly difficult to draw actors to these areas, over both the long- and short-term.

One artistic director from a theatre close to New York City argued that the energy of New York actors, whose craft is constantly honed by the competitiveness and variety of activity there, can be electrifying; he prefers casting each show out, rather than keeping a company in. Even among those artistic directors who want to maintain an acting company, many choose not to, preferring to cast each show individually, rather than to develop a company of severely limited size. While some artistic directors would leap at the chance of having a 15-person company, many others feel that anything less than 40 or 50 actors does not a company

make, and some would put the number at 100 or more. As one artistic
director argued, casting exclusively from a too small company always
involves using actors who are, at best, "least wrong for the most plays."
Another artistic director, who argued that a world-class acting company
needed a minimum of 40, described his ideal. The company would employ
100 actors of whom 30 to 40 might be on leave at any time; 20 actors
would regularly be on tour with a company production; the remaining 40
would be in residence, performing the season's work.

The American Conservatory Theatre (San Francisco) and the Guthrie
Theater (Minneapolis) in their early years assembled companies of
approximately 40, probably the largest corps of actors ever employed for
full seasons at American nonprofit theatres. This number would rank with
only the smallest European resident companies. Even the average ballet
and opera troupes in America have enough personnel to perform their
repertoires; American theatres, on the other hand, have to suit the
repertoire to the size of the company, instead of staffing in accordance
with the work they want to do. Indeed, a few artistic directors have
argued that even the most talented actors in small companies, who are
called upon to play lead roles in almost every show, can grow reliant on
old tricks, rather than exploring new territory, in order to handle the
grind of constant rehearsal and performance. Also, the small company
creates a sense of over-familiarity, in which audiences may get tired of
seeing the same actors so frequently. Although there are times in an
actor's career when continuous work is best, at other times this grind
can prove deeply detrimental, creating and reinforcing dangerous habits
and constricting an actor's imagination and spontaneity.

Artistic directors working with small resident companies (the only
kind that currently exist in America) are looking for ways to nurture the
actors in their companies -- to keep them growing without burning them
out. One artistic director argued that the best commitment a theatre
could make to the growth of an actor would be to promise four years of
work and then push the actor out of the nest to work with other people in
other theatres. Such movement between home theatres might begin to
establish a sort of floating ensemble. Other artistic directors are more
concerned with the ongoing training opportunities actors receive as part
of resident companies. They believe that the way to develop talent and
keep mature actors fresh is to supplement performance with classes and
workshops which allow actors to stretch and explore without the pressure
of an audience. Arena Stage (Washington, D.C.) has spent part of the
past three summers on retreat with its acting ensemble in Colorado,
developing new material and doing laboratory and class-work for actors.
Other artistic directors discussed the possibilities of running master
classes with guest artists, using senior actors as mentors for less
experienced ones. Still others raised the option of holding regular
movement and voice classes for company members to take advantage of as
they see fit. Several artistic directors imagined the creation of an
advanced training institute, where mature actors in mid-career could go
to hone their techniques, try new ways of approaching a role and
reenergize themselves, physically and vocally.

In addition to using training sessions to stretch and revitalize actors, many artistic directors agree that, like other artists working in the theatre, actors need more time. More rehearsal time, they believe, would certainly make actors more secure trying new things, working in ways that might feel odd and uncomfortable to them but which represent a stretch of their talents; too often, artistic directors fear, the imminence of performance pushes actors back on safe, habitual choices -- the things they know will "work" -- rather than encouraging new choices which would stimulate growth. Company members also need more time off. A year of constant rehearsal and performance (and rehearsal for a subsequent show during the run of a current one) is too much activity in too short a time, artistic directors agree. This squeeze of work practically eliminates the time actors need for relaxation, reflection and, perhaps most important, preparation for upcoming roles. Artistic directors suggest that time off between projects can be beneficial for the actor's growth.

Artistic directors of theatres that maintain resident acting companies are also looking for ways to involve those actors even more completely in the life of the institution and the community. They feel that actors are too often treated like children in need of pampering, rather than like responsible members of the theatre company. One suggestion arose that a theatre's repertoire might be determined in part by the needs of the actors in various stages of their growth, as often happens in older European companies with a cultivated sense of what role an actor requires to further his or her development at a given time. American Conservatory Theatre in San Francisco has an Artist Advisory Council that meets regularly with the artistic director. This council helps the artistic director formulate the theatre's five-year plans. The Guthrie Theater once maintained a four-actor committee that met regularly with the management, in order for them to understand management concerns and to bridge the gap between the artistic and management sides of the theatre. Other artistic directors are looking for ways to make interested visiting actors feel more involved in the theatre, by having them get to know the staff, learn how the theatre operates and meet on a regular basis with the resident artistic staff.

Attempts by theatres to integrate artists more completely underscore a major theme of artistic directors: the need to build relationships instead of merely writing contracts. The consensus was that healthy long-term relationships between artists and theatres help ensure better work by establishing common vocabularies; the theatre staff gets to know the way each artist works, what he or she needs and how best to compliment the artist's talents when putting together a team of collaborators. While a few artistic directors expressed concern that too many resident artists would cut further into the work available for freelance artists, numerous theatres already integrate writers, directors and designers into their institutional fabric and decision-making process through residencies and associate artist positions. These long-term full- or part-time relationships support the artists with money and time to work, and secure an artistic home-base. In exchange the theatres feel they can take advantage of these additional artistic voices for planning and can utilize the artist's expertise for other necessary services. Also, having artists in residence can allow theatres to work in new, more extended, more flexible ways, such as starting a designer's process well ahead of time or allowing a writer to have informal readings of a work in progress. Most important, the inclusion of other artists seems to create an exciting environment where art can grow. "When actors arrive and find a real sense of community among directors, dramaturgs and designers," one artistic director explained with enthusiasm, "they flourish. Having these artistic associates 'multiplies the joys and divides the griefs.'"

In companies with permanent acting ensembles, resident directors can develop a more continuous, organic relationship with the actors. Because a director in this situation would be familiar with the actors' patterns before embarking on a production, rehearsal time could be used more efficiently than when struggling with all unknown performers with different working methods and vocabularies. Some artistic directors who feel their theatres could flourish with the presence of other directors on staff caution that they would only be interested in directors who had equivalent or more experience than themselves. They want to surround themselves with equals, peers, not artists-in-training.

One artistic director suggested that residencies aren't structural but environmental: a way of creating the proper atmosphere for creativity to flourish. The structure of these residencies differs from theatre to theatre. Often they require no specific results from the artist, especially in the case of writers. Hartford Stage Company keeps a writer-in-residence without demanding any specific "product"; the arrangement is merely a long-term investment in this writer's talent. As it happens, except for one adaptation, the theatre has not yet produced this writer's original work on the main stage. While writing, she has served a dramaturgical function within the theatre -- sharing an expertise for working with other writers -- and, so, the investment has benefitted both the playwright and the theatre. Likewise, Baltimore's Center Stage has maintained two writers as artistic associates over a period of years. These two writers receive a stipend or fee but are not required to stay in residence nor to offer their plays to Center Stage. The theatre is under no obligation to produce them (though it has produced the work of both). Yet, the institution through these associate-ships serves as a sheltering home for these writers, providing some compensation and a safe place for their development and for their plays to be developed in workshops. A playwright in a theatre maintaining an acting company has the opportunity -- some would say advantage -- to write for a specific group of actors. At some theatres, a resident playwright, perhaps with a dramaturg, is a natural ambassador to the community. For the playwright, getting to know the theatre's community can provide context for plays and, moreover, insight into the audience these plays will address; for the community, meeting the playwright is a chance to find out more about the artistic processes of the theatre straight from an articulate and representative artist.

Many artistic directors seem particularly interested in bringing resident designers onto their staffs. They wish to hear the designer's voice in the process of planning seasons and to keep the design presence a part of early discussions of specific projects. Because of their constant research into other periods, designers are particularly well versed in history and related arts; they also, because of their ties to dance, music and fine arts, can bring new perspectives to the planning of theatre projects. Moreover, they can introduce artistic directors to other talented designers, of whom they may be unaware. A team of designers, working together through the course of a number of projects, according to artistic directors, can grow in exciting ways, merely by repeating the process regularly. In addition, the continued availability of the designer may allow the theatre to explore a design process different from the common kind, where designers do most of their work in isolation from the rehearsal process. The Wooster Group, for example, includes in the ensemble its resident designer, who is involved in rehearsals throughout the developmental process, as well as participating in the performances themselves. Missouri Repertory Theatre began the creation of a new version of Alice in Wonderland by giving designers a copy of the Lewis Carroll novel and asking them to design their own version of Wonderland, rather than starting with a directorial interpretation or dramatic text. The Goodman Theatre's recent production of She Always Said, Pablo culminated an uncommonly extended collaboration -- 10 years long -- that involved the design team with the director on a series of similar and related projects. It is interesting to note, though, that many designers prefer not to work over long periods of residency; as a result, they are sometimes perceived as a group to be the most remote members of the collaborative process.

Many artistic directors are enthusiastic about the creation of associate artistic director positions in their theatres. This title often applies to a full-time colleague -- most often, but not exclusively, another director -- who works with the artistic director on season planning, scouting, finding and developing projects, and who functions as a resident artist, doing his or her own work (e.g. directing plays) for the theatre. Usually, this person's tasks seem to be strictly artistic and free of the administrative detail that can bog artistic directors down. This freedom can allow the associate artistic director to concentrate on the kind of long-range development, such as overseeing commissions and projects in progress from which the artistic director sometimes gets deflected by the day-to-day demands of producing and responsibilities of running an institution. The associate artistic director also ensures the artistic director the consistent presence of another artistic mind off of which to bounce ideas. Ironically, many artistic directors consider this associate position -- with its freedom from institutional concern -- the most appealing job in their theatres, including their own.

Goodman Theatre (Chicago) with two associate directors, each directing one show a season (the artistic director directs a third one) is exploring the new flexibility that this tripartite arrangement might be able to give its operations. Already this structure relieves the artistic director from sole responsibility for picking a season; each director chooses the piece he wants to work on, thereby guaranteeing a season of personal, idiosyncratic productions. In the future, a structure like this could conceivably rotate in a way that would free each artist up to concentrate wholly on artistic work at some times and on managing the artistic resources of the theatre at others. The variations on effective new structures involving associate artistic directors are endless.

On the subject of residencies and artistic associates, artistic directors are convinced that the presence of other artists would never water down their leadership, any more than the involvement of senior managers, consultants and advisors water down the management of a corporation or agency. Rather, they feel that this involvement will help them get the information they need to fulfill their visions and make the best possible decisions. In fact, a few have noted that associates sometimes feel, based on the decisions artistic directors ultimately make, that their advice isn't taken into account fully; these artistic directors want to find ways of making it clear to associates that they do take this advice seriously, that it influences their thinking, and that, in most cases, these ideas significantly affect the decision-making process, even though the ideas themselves may not always be implemented directly.

4. <u>There is a need to invest in the future of the art form and the profession by taking responsibility for the training of and access for future artists and nontraditional artists, including minority and women artists.</u>

Something serious is lacking in the training of American theatre artists, artistic directors almost unanimously agree: a commitment to theatre as a profession. Most graduates of the nation's training programs, according to artistic directors, no longer aspire to careers on the stage; they no longer see life in a resident company as a sufficient goal. The possibilities for fame and financial windfalls in television and film have supplanted those goals for the young actor. In the TCG meetings, artistic directors probed their own responsibility for the current situation and considered possible solutions to this deficiency, a problem that they fear could cut the American theatre off from its own future.

Artistic directors mostly agree that the conduit between training programs and professional theatres has been severed. Many of the nation's resident theatres were initially homes for actors who came out of school together; in some instances these groups of artists actually formed the theatre. As the theatres have grown up, however, and the generations of artists who founded them have matured, access to theatres for current graduates has been drastically reduced. Partly, this reflects an increased professionalism and quality in the work of the theatres, which now have access to more experienced actors and are reluctant to make efforts to develop young talent. Artistic directors agree: The theatre doesn't provide jobs to enough young artists.

When the regional theatres started forming, virtually all expected to soon be working in repertory, which would demand building a resident company. They needed, therefore, a way of hiring beginning actors at lower rates than experienced ones, to play small roles and develop as future company members. This led to the formation of a new Actors' Equity Association contract (the LORT contract), which made it possible for young actors to join companies as journeymen on a seasonal basis for lower salaries. Once theatres abandoned the company concept and started hiring show by show, this contract provision eroded. Fulltime apprenticeships and intern programs for young professionals are now very limited, reducing the possibility of a more gradual, progressive development of young actors. In the meantime, the availability to young actors of lucrative and prestigious work in film and television has made these venues accessible to people straight out of school (and sometimes to those still in school). Moreover, with debts from four years or more of paying high tuitions (which continue to rise), most students simply can't afford the kind of alternative lifestyle that waiting to break into theatre -- and make some semblance of a living from it -- demands. Concurrently, theatre programs have broadened their focus. As funding to education was cut in the late '70s and early '80s, along with that to the arts, heads of acting programs increasingly had to justify their programs to the universities on the basis of employment statistics -- not the quality of training. Artistic directors see the result of these trends as an over-emphasis on success in the job market, especially television and commercial media.

This grim situation is worsened by the rift and mutual distrust between academic theatre and the profession, a rift that only a few artistic directors say they work actively to bridge. Many artistic directors believe that with a few important exceptions American training programs are out of touch with the theatrical process; that they over-simplify training, as if theatre were merely about "doing shows"; that they're "packaging" students as personalities for media acceptance, rather than readying them for the craft demands of the stage. Overall, artistic directors fear that educators and students now see work in the theatre, once the ultimate goal of these training programs, as a last resort.

Artistic directors voice many specific complaints about the training young artists receive, which they say usually gives students neither specific technical grounding in their craft nor a rigorous, intellectual process. For instance, they mostly agree that no proper course of study for directors exists -- or can exist; learning to direct is a life-long process, but students leave school thinking they are ready to direct. Another concern is that designers are not taught enough about the process of directing, and this lack of understanding can lead designers to distrust directors, rather than to collaborate with them. Actor training, most artistic directors agreed, tends to emphasize such job-skills classes as auditioning and "On-camera Techniques," while paying short shrift to the kind of vocal and physical training that all actors need for a life in the theatre.

At one meeting, artistic directors discussed rallying together to write an open letter, outlining the ways educational institutions have failed the theatre. Many artistic directors, though, strongly blame themselves for remaining aloof from the educational process, and for failing to participate in the training and entry-level hiring of future artists. All over the world, artistic directors explained, their peers take responsibility for training in addition to their own artistic work. Many American artistic directors, on the other hand, censure themselves for cutting ties with universities and conservatories and for not pursuing new alliances with them. One artistic director suggested that the theatres should take the lead in identifying exciting teachers and find ways of getting them into the schools, even on a workshop or master class basis; exciting teachers inspire students to want to be involved with theatre, he argued. Those artistic directors who believe that actors must be trained in theatres and not in schools, hold themselves especially accountable for the lack of apprenticeship opportunities provided by their theatres. Likewise, they acknowledge the decline of entry-level opportunities for directors; the practical experience directors need in order to continue their training and segue into professional careers -- including the chance to watch other directors at work -- is virtually unavailable in nonprofit theatres.

A number of artistic directors look to models from other countries for a way out of this dilemma. In Canada, for instance, artistic directors at theatres funded by the federal government used to be required to put time into teaching or directing at the National Theatre School on a regular basis. In Finland, according to one artistic director, the heads of theatres don't wait until the training is over to observe the actors' work; they enter the process in the middle of the program, and so become invested in the students' growth. Other countries have consistent apprenticeship programs that work young talents into companies and allow them to continue training, as well as to observe more experienced artists in action.

Here in America a few theatres currently work hand in hand with university training programs. Yale Repertory Theatre (New Haven, Conn.) and American Repertory Theatre (Cambridge, Mass.) are supported in part by the universities that house them -- Yale and Harvard. Students study and work side by side with theatre professionals, and young artists have regular opportunities to apprentice or perform with senior artists. (Yale also trains a number of theatre administrators, who hold positions at the Rep during their third year.) Likewise, Missouri Repertory Theatre is tied to the University of Missouri in Kansas City and oversees the training. Third-year actors in the Master of Fine Arts program are required to spend a season in residence at the theatre, where they must understudy or play small roles. An understudy performance is scheduled for each show, so that all student actors appear before an audience in

the roles for which they have been standing by. Similarly, PlayMakers
Repertory Company offers contracts to third-year students from the
University of North Carolina at Chapel Hill, with whose training program
it is affiliated.

Other theatres operate training programs independent of universities
or other institutions. American Conservatory Theatre in San Francisco
maintains one of the oldest conservatory programs in the country. There
is a great deal of crossover between the conservatory and the theatre --
the theatre's artists teaching at the school and the students working
with the theatre company. A small group of theatres are considering a
collaborative effort to contract third-year students from each other's
training programs. Under such an arrangement, Alliance Theatre (Atlanta)
could provide a year of professional experience for the graduating class
of Denver Center Theatre Company's conservatory, for example. Other
theatres in non-theatre centers must provide work and classes to
cultivate the local talent pool, a process that can take many years.
Berkeley Repertory Theatre (California) has organized a second company
of local, non-Equity talent to perform touring shows and outreach
projects, while serving as understudies and walk-ons in mainstage
productions. These company members, in addition to earning $175 a week,
earn Equity Membership Candidate points, making them union members after
the two-year program.

Just as artistic directors agree that they have taken too little
responsibility nationally for the training of future artists, they
adamantly concur that they and their institutions have generally done far
too little to promote and provide access for minority, ethnic and (until
recently, some argue) women artists. This issue arose most often out of
discussions of "non-traditional casting," in which minority actors and
women are cast in roles where race, gender or ethnicity aren't germane to
a play's story. Nevertheless, the consensus clearly arose that such
efforts must apply to writers, designers, directors and administrators as
well. Three arguments recurred most often among artistic directors: 1)
We must provide more and more equal employment for minority artists in
the theatres; 2) Only by opening the theatres to more diverse artists can
the theatre hope to again become relevant to the world around us -- a
racially mixed, interdependent world; and 3) Theatres must provide more
culturally varied experiences on stage than it currently does if they
hope to attract new, ethnically diverse audiences. Certainly, artistic
directors realize that the support of women and minority artists is more
than a gesture towards "affirmative action" hiring; it is, many believe,
an initiative necessary for the survival of the theatre as a vital,
relevant art form. This initiative will take, they feel, commitment from
the theatre community at all levels, beginning with the will to look at
the ethnic composition of play casts in new and imaginative ways, and
including the dedication to produce work that draws on the experiences of
many cultures and races and provides more employment opportunities for
minority actors.

The concern that most minority artists haven't received adequate
training was countered by the insistence that giving these artists more

work will make them better. The theatres themselves may have to make a
concerted effort to cultivate and provide opportunities for this talent,
artistic directors say, as they have done with local acting pools. One
artistic director exclaimed, "We have to do it and be more aggressive
about it. If there is an issue to go down fighting for, this is it!" In
fact, Milwaukee Repertory Theater's experience of the past two seasons
should demonstrate that nontraditional casting initiatives do not
jeopardize a theatre's survival. On the contrary, since Milwaukee Rep
became the first major regional theatre to institute an across-the-board
color-blind casting policy, hiring five minority actors for its twelve-
member company and producing an entire second stage season of plays
written or co-written by black writers, its audience has expanded.

OUR AUDIENCE OURSELVES

"We beat ourselves too much about audiences; the
majority of people have always been drawn to popular
entertainment. Most of Shakespeare's audience
preferred bear-baiting."

-- Robert Falls
Artistic Director
Goodman Theatre

"I'm increasingly frightened by the audience because
the most popular work is not the work closest to me."

-- Russell Vandenbroucke
Artistic Director
Northlight Theatre

The responsibility artistic directors feel toward their audiences is
one part of a complex set of responsibilities which often operate in
tension with each other. As one artistic director put it, they must
serve numerous interests: 1) themselves as artists, 2) other artists, 3)
their audiences, 4) the community at large and 5) the art form in general.
While each theatre would order these priorities differently, and would
probably reorder them for each specific project, the struggle to find
balance among them is a major concern of the nation's artistic leaders.

The responsibility to audiences creates one of the more pressing
questions artistic directors face: how to strike a balance between two
extremes -- their responsibility to their own artistic fulfillment and
the pressure to fill the theatre with a satisfied audience, getting what it
wants? Certainly, no single answer exists. In fact, artistic directors
don't even agree about the nature of the problem. Some resent the fact
that theatre is the one art form expected to fulfill a popular role as
entertainment; they resist the phrase "show business" and seek a way to
market the art, not just the package of individual productions. One such
artistic director described choosing plays according to what audiences
"should see" as "a bloodless form of self-censorship." Others believe
that theatre is first and foremost obligated to please a broad audience
and that without such an audience there can be no theatre. To these
artistic directors, the unwillingness of less pragmatic leaders to pay
more attention to the market potential of their work appears naive. This
difference of opinion was illustrated in the following interchange: one
artistic director, who believes that "If you trust the artist, you'll
find the audience," was answered by another: "I no longer believe
audiences will come to see our best work; we can't always get the

audience we deserve."

Other artistic directors argue that vital theatre comes out of the needs of a specific community, that it exists to excite and enrich that community and, so, it is unwise to look at a theatre's agenda separately from that of the community as a whole. What a community needs, as opposed to what it thinks it wants, might be determined instinctively or empathetically by the artist, some believe. One artistic director expressed the belief that artists are "guardians, preservers of the culture and heritage," who, doing the work of the storyteller, "define, challenge and maintain the values of society by telling tales from the culture." Still others avoid addressing this question in general terms, insisting that the balance of these responsibilities must be determined on a project-by-project basis.

Whatever their side of this volatile issue, artistic directors are all looking for ways of overcoming a sense of alienation from their audiences and from the people who aren't attending the theatre at all. Often, they question themselves: "Are we underestimating our audiences by holding back more challenging work? Does our work lack quality?" Many artistic directors answer yes to both questions. One artistic director summed up the sentiment of many: "Sometimes we just don't do what we do well enough. We have an obligation to do it better." Whatever the cause, artistic directors agree that the Broadway theatre establishment is not interested in audience development, believing that "hits" are sufficient to bring people to the theatre, and that it is therefore up to the nonprofit community to cultivate theatre audiences.

Essentially, the tension between the artist and his or her audience is a programming issue: Should artistic directors choose seasons based on their own needs and instincts as artists or based on what they feel their audience should see or would come to see? The answer seems partly to depend on location. In areas with only one theatre, for example, it has been argued that the theatre has a responsiblity to present a broad-ranging repertoire, to acquaint its audience with the whole of theatre as an art form through "the standard repertoire" (i.e. important contemporary plays, regular helpings of Shakespeare and world classics, selections from different eras and styles -- a menu of the theatre's representative fare). Theatres in areas with substantial activity, where the standard repertoire is spread out over a number of theatres, are somewhat freer to produce a narrower, more alternative program, and, in so doing, reflect the tastes and interests of a single artistic leader. For instance, because one theatre is serving a large community with a broad and representative world repertoire, a neighboring theatre in the same town might concentrate on new plays and experimental productions of world classics. Although such examples are not clear-cut, they represent two distinct (albeit hypothetical) approaches to programming: one in which the audience's needs are put first in the selection of a season; the other, the artist's needs. Most seasons are selected with a mixture of concerns in mind. At one meeting, an artistic director suggested that this growing sense of obligation to program for the audience would be different if Broadway were still vital; the nonprofit theatres, he suggested, have to some degree, "lost the luxury of being alternative" and, so, become the mainstream.

Artistic directors at the TCG meetings sent out a mixed message: Many are afraid of being forced to program two seasons each year -- the one they pick for themselves hidden in the one they program for the audience; yet most feel they are currently choosing the seasons they want, unconstrained by the demands of the audience. On the one hand, they are saying they do the work they want to do; on the other hand, they worry that they have gotten so good at accepting limitations on their work -- such as the need to "fund-raise at the box office" by choosing plays with popular appeal, and to accede to the budgetary restrictions which limit cast size and the scale of production -- that they may have lost track of what they want to do. The desire to satisfy some idea of what the audience will like and the ability to constrict their imaginations to work within institutional limits are, artistic directors fear, subtle and dangerous forms of self-censorship. As one artistic director put it, "Sometimes I listen to my voice and I can't tell how many compromises I'm speaking out of." In a sense, all artistic directors are looking for ways to expand their audiences that won't alter their own artistic programs. For many, the ideal would allow them to challenge theatregoers (and themselves) more, censor themselves less and develop larger, more loyal audiences.

1. <u>Artistic directors want to expand theatre audiences to include members of the community who don't traditionally subscribe and those who rarely attend, without jeopardizing their personal artistic visions.</u>

Many artistic directors fear that they rely too heavily on a single audience, a fairly homogeneous group, usually subscribers. This audience tends to consist of white, middle-class, educated people over 45, usually raised on theatregoing, financially secure with some disposable income and a propensity towards planning their activities in advance. According to artistic directors, this group, and their audience in general, is getting older, while dance and performance art are drawing younger audiences. As they witness the aging of this subscription group, artistic directors worry because they see no clear successors, no new generations of subscribers at hand.

While they almost unanimously value and depend on their subscribers, many artistic directors lament the fact that their audience does not more clearly reflect the demographics of society, including younger people and people from the range of minority and ethnic groups that make up American culture. They feel a need to address the concerns of these diverse segments of society and to build a varied and continuing audience to augment the current, finite one. It may well be, as artistic directors occasionally argued, that the potential audience for theatre is finite, and that theatre is, in some way, an elitist or non-democratic activity; nonetheless, all agreed that even if the possible audience is limited, it is not limited to a particular class, race or age group. Whatever the theoretical potential may be, the theatres' welfare depends on cultivating a broader pool from which to draw audiences for different types of work. Simply put, artistic directors feel the need to get more people into the theatre. The audience they want is made up of many audiences.

The current methods of audience development are geared primarily toward the subscriber or potential subscriber. Schedules are set and the audience is expected to plan well ahead to reserve space for approximately six different offerings. Again, this program fits perfectly into one kind of life, but many people -- especially in a culture revolving more and more around impulse buying -- resist such regimentation and forethought. In fact, more than one artistic director suggested that theatres asking anyone to come six times a year may be asking too much, that so heavy a schedule can either make the theatre-going experience begin to seem mundane or foster in the subscriber a sense of ownership of the theatre which, when voiced, adds weight to the obligation the artistic director feels about giving the audience what it wants. A group of artistic directors speculated that the current structure has also created around theatre-going a sense of formality alien to many people, who might drop by a restaurant or movie on the spur of the moment, but are convinced that good theatre is always sold out ahead of time. In the end, many performances wind up with empty seats, some of the vacancies left by subscribers themselves who don't show up and don't exchange their reservations for another night. Some large theatres have almost 1,000 seats a week that are sold, but not filled. Artistic directors want to be able to fill those seats, but are at a loss to figure out how. The Old Globe Theatre (San Diego) is experimenting with selling these vacant seats at discounted rates. Patrons at sold-out performances buy "Flex-tix," which entitle them to stand through a play's first scene and then take empty seats for the remainder of the show; these tickets differ from traditional standing-room passes in that the audience member may return them for a full refund if no seats become available and he or she prefers not to stand throughout the performance.

The practices of subscription, upon which so many nonprofit theatres depend, don't always work for small theatres tending to maintain more flexible seasons. It is sometimes difficult for less-established theatres to offer a half-year ahead of time the four, five or six shows necessary to comprise an attractive subscription offering; too often they need a more flexible schedule in order to capitalize on successful shows, or they simply can't afford to do the advance planning necessary to consolidate and promote a season early enough to sell it. Furthermore, for theatres without a great deal of marketing sophistication, subscription programs can drain too much time and money. These theatres haven't found alternative ways of ensuring audiences and of keeping the house full in early weeks of a run (usually filled by subscribers at larger theatres) before word-of-mouth on a show gets going. In addition, as one artistic director explained, the number of subscribers to a theatre is sometimes used by funders in their decision-making process -- as if quantity were the standard of excellence.

Many artistic directors feel the need to explore new ways of getting non-subscribers and single-ticket buyers into the theatres on a regular basis. In fact, while the lack of startling new ideas for building audiences concerns them, they believe that audience development requires continual work and innovation on all fronts. They seek a way of balancing subscription benefits with the incentives available to non-subscribers. In other words, they are looking for a way to make theatre more attractive to people who don't want to subscribe, without weakening the appeal for those who do. Holding on to the audience they have is a prime concern among artistic directors, and, therefore, they find the subscriber who drops out, who makes a decision to stop coming, the most worrisome. The smaller the community and the more limited the potential audience, the more dangerous such desertion seems, a situation that makes it even harder to take risks that might alienate current audiences. If the potential audience is small, few people get to see even the best work. As one artistic director said, "There are a lot of trees falling and no one's hearing them." Since the size of an audience is limited only within a given place, the suggestion was made that co-productions or tours of shows from one nonprofit theatre to others can enhance the audience for any given production.

In larger communities, risky programming choices can have strong impact on audience development. American Repertory Theatre (Cambridge, Mass.) and Alley Theatre (Houston) have proved that challenging and unexpected material can indeed build audiences, even on the main stage and through subscription marketing. A.R.T. reconstituted virtually its entire subscription audience, alienating their early audiences by producing the work of avant-garde directors, who boldly experimented with classic plays; once more than half of this audience had fled, a new, larger one, more attuned to the theatre's aesthetic, took its place. A.R.T. built this new audience by focusing not on the people who had left but on those who had stayed.   Last season the Alley Theatre, which had for many years responded to its audience's existing tastes, produced David Mamet's Glengarry Glen Ross and Sam Shepard's Lie of the Mind back to back.   They provoked letters of protest from some subscribers, but they also attracted huge single-ticket sales and a younger audience. Lie virtually sold out with audiences who, despite the show's length -- nearly four hours -- stayed to the end, thereby defying popular wisdom that no one will sit in the theatre for longer than two hours anymore. Several artistic directors argued that only by doing more challenging work, including work that integrates new technology with theatre design and performance, can theatres draw younger audiences. Many theatres have already found this to be true; by scheduling plays of limited or unusual appeal in their second stage series, they have attracted new audience groups, other than their usual subscribers.

Many theatres have lately experimented with flexible passes in place of subscriptions in hopes of appealing to audiences unwilling to plan far ahead.   Both the New York Shakespeare Festival and Lincoln Center Theatre operate on this system. Generally, the purchase of these passes entitles holders to reserve and buy discounted tickets for each production closer to the actual run, instead of months in advance, giving them the benefit of more spontaneity in scheduling. For the theatre, the pass system offers the advantage of postponing the announcement of specific titles and dates until nearer the opening and minimizes the hassle of accommodating subscribers wishing to exchange tickets for days other than the ones they originally committed to. Unfortunately, many artistic directors have been less than optimistic about the results. Because passes still require some up-front costs, they seem to attract the same people as subscriptions, rather than bringing in new audiences. Focus groups at Los Angeles Theatre Works, for example, found that most pass-buyers were heavy subscribers, who attended many arts events and rarely went to the movies. In addition, many among them had trouble with the passes, specifically because the traditional subscriber wants to be able to plan in advance. The Mark Taper Forum (Los Angeles) also found the pass system disappointing. Passholders behaved like single-ticket buyers, waiting for good reviews before reserving seats or not purchasing the discounted tickets at all, thus jeopardizing box office projections. Moreover, without the discipline of having to plan the season well ahead, the artistic staff found itself growing increasingly lax and less committed to the necessary work of long-range planning.

Of course, the most difficult issue in recent audience development efforts, the one most pertinent to a theatre's artistic program, is how to reach the people who never come to the theatre. Virginia Stage Company is exploring the use of task forces of non-audience members working with the theatre to find out why people don't come to the theatre, what can be done to get them there and how to keep them coming back. Other artistic leaders are looking at the relatively homogenous cultural make-up of their audiences and wondering how they can alter them to reflect the diversity of the community around them.

Artistic directors are especially determined to change the ethnic content of their audiences by reaching out to minority communities who rarely or never attend. As with the inclusion of nontraditional artists in the theatre, many view the integration of theatre audiences as a necessity. They insist that only by more fully representing the ethnic diversity of American life and culture, both onstage and in the house, can theatre hope to remain a vital and relevant part of that culture. Again, such attempts require longterm initiative and continual innovation. Mostly, though, artistic directors agree, they require the will and commitment to change. "If you want minority audiences or young audiences," one artistic director declared, "you've got to pay, and it's got to be someone's job to get them." When the Mark Taper Forum hired an anthropologist as associate artistic director, his job included finding ways to involve Los Angeles's large Hispanic community in the theatre. Some of his subsequent discoveries helped the theatre develop that new audience through relatively simple steps, including: the establishment of a babysitting service in the theatre, for parents who couldn't afford to pay for both babysitters and tickets, and a change in advertising practices -- such as putting up posters in the community when it was found that these audiences didn't pay attention to newspaper reviews.

Only clearly targeted efforts succeed, many artistic directors believe. These efforts, they explain, are partly marketing-oriented and partly environmental; the very buildings that theatres are housed in, sometimes associated with elitism and wealth, can seem uninviting. The theatres which have attracted new, more diverse audiences have done so through a combination of efforts. The New York Shakespeare Festival, for instance, has for years maintained a heavily integrated audience through a demonstrated commitment to ethnic and minority writers and their plays, interracial casting, and outreach programs citywide, including those designed to bring theatre to urban children. For almost a decade the Goodman Theatre (Chicago) has made great strides toward building a new audience through a combination of interracial casting, producing plays by minority writers, booking in tours of plays by blacks and through grassroots marketing efforts in Chicago's ethnic communities.

Some fear that presenting work of more ethnic appeal will have an adverse effect on current audiences. Yet Milwaukee Repertory Theater has found that its new program of color-blind casting, coupled with a commitment to black writers, has increased its audiences without diminishing its largely Caucasian base of habitual subscribers.

A number of theatres have proved that attracting minority audiences is an artistic issue; the plays a theatre chooses to produce can make a significant difference in the cultural make-up of its audience. The Negro Ensemble Company (New York City) has helped boost black attendance at theatres across the country by circulating national touring companies of such acclaimed shows as Home and A Soldier's Play. The critical and box office success of these productions -- in addition to the heavy attendance of black audiences primarily for black musicals on Broadway -- has sent strong signals to theatres that minority audiences exist and that they will attend theatre if the theatres show an interest in their art and culture. Los Angeles Theatre Center has made attracting minority audiences an artistic priority. By producing plays by black and Hispanic writers as an integral part of each mainstage season, LATC has attested to the importance of cultural diversity; as a result, the theatre has changed the mix of its audiences to include 4,000 black subscribers in a total of 28,000. The Old Globe Theatre (San Diego) and South Coast Repertory (Costa Mesa, Calif.) have both found that cross-cultural programming can attract new audiences. By supporting Hispanic writers through special play development and workshop programs and, more important, by producing these writers' work on their main stages, these two theatres have changed the composition of their audiences to better reflect the ethnic mix of southern California. A number of theatres specialize in ethnic or multicultural work or the work of special concerns, including: Pan Asian Repertory Theatre, Honolulu Theatre for Youth, The Mixed Blood Theatre Company, At the Foot of the Mountain, Repertorio Espanol and AMAS Repertory Theatre.

Most theatres hope to draw a younger audience as well, in order to begin developing the audience of the future. Yet many artistic directors speculate that theatre is too expensive to attract price-sensitive and younger people. They have found that the age of an audience is influenced by the cost of a ticket. As a result, many theatres have experimented with lower ticket prices, including half-price "rush" tickets available the day of performance. La Jolla Playhouse offered a "pay what you can" subscription series for Saturday matinees. Hartford Stage Company even tried selling $2.00 tickets through community outreach programs. Across the country preview audiences are younger, because tickets are cheaper. Arena Stage (Washington, D.C.) introduced a $10 standing-room ticket for Yuri Lyubimov's recent production of Crime and Punishment. They advertised these low-price tickets and began accepting reservations; tickets sold at half-price -- $5.00 -- during previews. This experiment brought long lines of 20- to 35-year-olds to the theatre. It was so successful that Arena plans to continue the practice. This under-40 age group is the one artistic directors miss most in their theatres. A number of artistic directors feel that the 35- to 45-year-old generation is basically lost to the theatre, that the theatre hasn't been provocative or relevant enough to attract either the generation that has grown up on film and television, or another, younger group, currently drawn to MTV. Although a few artistic directors feel cautiously optimistic that a younger audience is starting to attend, most feel that a great deal more needs to be done to secure for the theatre younger audiences for now and any audiences for the future.

2. <u>Theatres need to take the initiative to develop and educate future audiences.</u>

Most artistic directors look for tomorrow's audience in today's classroom. They agree that it is the responsibility of the theatre community to condition audiences from school age on to see the theatre as an important part of their lives. Moreover, many find in schools, especially high schools, genuinely exciting audiences, who, in one artistic director's words, "get everything." Since funds for federal arts in education programs have been curtailed under the Reagan Administration, theatres, in partnership with local governments, are having to rebuild programs to get schools into the theatres and theatres into schools. These initiatives, many artistic directors agree, are difficult to make into high priorities because they are so long-range. Nevertheless, they insist, the development of these future audiences is a survival issue; it must be made a priority.

One artistic director spoke for many when he said, "We must get students to the theatre, not just the other way around." Certainly, the best arrangement for educating future audiences about the theatre is to let them see it firsthand: viewing plays, meeting artists, touring the stage and behind the scenes. Many theatres throughout the nation schedule regular student matinees of their mainstage plays. Others mount plays exclusively for a student audience, often utilizing acting apprentices and second companies. Last year, the New York Shakespeare Festival inaugurated a full repertory season and theatre company to perform for New York inner city school children. The Festival took over the Belasco Theatre, a little-used Broadway house, negotiated a set of unique union contracts, and hired an ensemble of actors to mount a rotating repertory season of three Shakespeare plays, which they performed at a rate of 10 a week for thousands of school children. American Conservatory Theatre (San Francisco) is another example of a theatre with a large-scale education season. With support from PepsiCo, they present nearly 30 student matinees a year. Los Angeles Theatre Center emphasizes theatre's role as a tool for learning. The theatre staff holds mandatory six-hour workshops for teachers before they bring students to a performance. In return, the teachers commit to at least one hour of teaching about the play, which will result in specific student creations, such as poems or works of art inspired by their theatregoing experience. One theatre actually utilizes students as spokespeople for audience development; the theatre offers free tickets when these children escort their parents to the theatre. Trinity Repertory Company (Providence, R.I.) has been working with school children for 20 years. This theatre currently reaps the rewards: many of these children are adult subscribers now, and they bring their own children with them.

It is, however, often more feasible to bring the theatre to the students than otherwise. A small group of actors, for example, can travel more easily and cheaply than hundreds of students; moreover, out in the schools, a theatre can reach more students than it would be possible to bring into the theatre. In addition to touring productions to the schools, many theatres have developed programs which make the theatre experience an integral part of the educational process. Living Stage Theatre Company (Washington, D.C.) has been creating plays with special populations -- including disadvantaged children, drug abusers and prisoners -- for over 30 years. Intiman Theatre Company (Seattle) has a residency program that sends actors into history and literature classes. There they do improvisations around the theatre's productions of classic plays, leading students through an investigation of the play's period. The students ask questions of characters in the plays, as well as working on characters themselves. Teaching tools like this provide information while revealing the process of theatre. Another Seattle theatre, Seattle Repertory Theatre, commissions a play each year specifically to bring into the schools, thereby involving writers in the educational process. Los Angeles Theatre Works is working with juvenile court schools in the Los Angeles area. In this way, the theatre can involve hundreds of difficult and "special needs" children in arts workshops. Theatre Project Company (St. Louis) has used similar workshops as research for creation of theatre pieces, such as the recent project on the subject of teenage pregnancy. These programs and others like them are, artistic directors believe, the basis for both exciting theatre projects today and exciting theatre audiences tomorrow.

"For me, 'institution' is the most wonderful word and the
scariest. Whoever would have thought 25 years ago, when
we started these theatres, that we'd be sitting
together now, talking about our institutions?"

-- Gordon Davidson
Artistic Director/Producer
Mark Taper Forum

"An institution cannot have a life of its own, be a
thing in itself. Its life is derived from the
animating idea, and each and every one of its actions
must flow from this idea and contain a piece of it.
When we say 'the business of art is art and not
business,' we don't mean there is no business in making
art (surely there is!) but that the function and
purpose of the business is not itself, but the making
of this art."

-- Zelda Fichandler
Producing Director
Arena Stage

The foundations of America's institutional theatres are lodged in
shifting ground. Whereas the majority of theatres have been led during
the past two or three decades by their founding artistic directors,
working with manager-partners and boards which they recruited and
developed, many theatres have recently undergone or are currently
undergoing changes in artistic leadership. In fact, a number of theatres
have changed artistic directors three or more times.

Other theatres find their relationship to the community changed by
the acquisition of real estate. Theatres started in found spaces --
churches, schools or public buildings -- solicit capital to build or
acquire facilities of their own; theatres with one space seek to add
others or to create theatre centers around themselves. Theatres
acquiring new or expanded facilities need new levels of financial, legal
and political support. Their boards and audiences often reconstitute as
a result. In fact, their relationship to the entire community changes.
Almost all theatres have altered the way they present themselves to their
communities and the way they do business, by adding increasingly
sophisticated management systems for marketing, accounting and fund-
raising. In short, theatres that started as ideas in the minds of one
person or a small group of people have blossomed into major institutions

housed in buildings held in trust by large boards and operated with a kind of business savvy which would have been inconceivable even a decade ago.

Certainly, not all theatres have burgeoned in exactly the same way. Some have worked to stay small. Others have remained collective in their decision-making process, groups of artists bringing on administrators and managers to assist them. Some theatres rely on joint artistic leaders and no managing director; others are run by producers who also direct, some by those who don't. Many theatres move from performance space to performance space, avoiding the problems of ownership, although few have been exempt from the problems of tight and expensive real estate markets, whether they are sometime-renters or buyers.

Despite these differences, relationships between those who run theatres have changed and continue to do so, throughout the field. Regularly, where artistic leadership has passed from founders to members of a new generation of artistic directors, boards have been called upon to hire new artistic leaders; in the past, it was the artistic leadership who recruited trustees. Real estate has brought to the nonprofit theatre the complications of ownership, where boards of trustees[*], with their signatures on loans and leases, become legally and financially responsible for institutions to a greater extent than ever before. While no individuals actually own nonprofit theatres, the increased responsibility can create a sense of ownership which, along with the new responsibility to hire artistic directors -- and thereby influence greatly the ultimate artistic direction of the theatre -- has the potential to skew what is essentially a partnership of colleagues. The previous system of an enterprise run by co-equals in service of an artistic idea is replaced with an employer-employee relationship where artistic directors serve at the pleasure of their boards. The inequality of this new relationship reinforces a cultural perception under which artistic directors feel they sometimes labor, the perception of business people and trustees as adults who do "real work" and artists as children who merely play.

As the business demands on theatres have become more stringent, the responsiblities of management have grown increasingly demanding and complex. As theatres expanded from their beginnings as artistic collectives, there was a concommitant (and necessary) growth in management; recognizing the need for administrative expansion if theatres were to survive as institutions, theatres staffed accordingly. Generally speaking, they were transformed from companies of artists -- especially as resident acting ensembles began to be abandoned in favor of freelance

----

[*]

The use of the phrase "board of trustees" is widely preferred among artistic directors over "board of directors." They mostly agree that it more accurately reflects the duties of the board, and its relationship to the theatre, which they hold in trust, rather than "direct."

hiring of artists -- to companies predominated by administrators. This transformation altered the theatres' loyalties as well; it became more incumbent on the theatres' leaders to support dedicated, permanent employees (primarily administrative staff) as opposed to part-time labor (primarily artists). Moreover, freelance costs have always been easier to control than staff salaries. It is simpler to scale down production costs -- by doing smaller cast shows, for example -- than it is to cut fulltime staff members, who are part of the daily life of the theatre and whose interests are, therefore, more regularly voiced. The duties of artistic directors have, likewise, grown more demanding and complex, but theatres have, on the whole, not allowed for equivalent artistic expansion, even though it is the artistic work which ultimately determines success or failure.

The growing split between artistic and management functions and the resultant division of labor between artists and managers has changed the terms of their partnership. The environment for theatre has thus become increasingly "corporate." Fierce marketing, public relations and fund-raising competition have required artists to constantly re-articulate the value of their art to a greater number of funders and others. As a result, artists in the theatres often spend as much time selling the work as doing it. This perpetual salesmanship has intensified the need for them to speak the language of business both inside and outside their theatres, something they have obviously learned to do quite well.

Once business becomes the language of the theatre, though, the artistic endeavor, rather than being sustained by the business, is in danger of being called upon to sustain it. A theatre's artistic needs can seem vague and impractical in relation to the requirements of the "bottom line." Business psychology wants results not process, a frame of mind that can lead to equating artistic success with box office hits. This bottom-line mentality perpetuates a sad irony of theatre funding: even businesses which understand their own need for research and development don't understand the need for it in the theatre. The natural affinity between boards and managers -- natural because trustees are often managers in their own professions -- is able to flourish under such circumstances, while artistic directors, often with only a single voice to express their concerns, can begin to appear less relevant. What starts as a harmony of strong voices -- artistic, management and community -- has the potential of losing the proper blend.

The danger, many artistic directors feel, is that the artist-manager partnership will also be thrown off balance. Artistic directors want to fend off any further separation between art and business, to eliminate any "we" vs. "they" spirit that might exist between artists and managers, or artists and trustees. In theatres with new artistic directors, managing directors are often the people on staff with the longest tenure and often the ones who have kept the theatre alive through a difficult transition period. Some have been given new titles to reflect their additional responsibilities during these periods, such as producing director or executive director. The manager is called upon during such times to be the sole spokesperson of the theatre, a position ideally belonging to the artistic director or shared between artistic and managing directors. Creating a new partnership, one that acknowledges the experience and profound investment of the manager while ensuring that business structures follow rather than precede the theatre's new artistic vision, can be tricky. Managers and boards of trustees are likely to be their most skittish during such transitions at exactly the time the new artistic director is the least confident and informed; nevertheless, this is the point at which artistic directors feel it is most necessary to reaffirm the precedence of the artistic idea and to reestablish theatre buildings as artistic homes.

1. Artistic directors need to communicate more effectively with their boards of trustees and work with them to reevaluate board structures, and to make sure these structures serve the artistic mission, especially in theatres with new artistic directors and longer-lived trustees.

The National Artistic Agenda Project grew out of a need for better communication between artistic directors and their boards. As Peter Zeisler explains in his introduction, trustees felt that artistic directors could help them serve the theatres' guiding visions more effectively if they had a clear sense of specific artistic needs. The trustees' request has triggered self-questioning among artistic leaders about what they expect from boards and how they can work better with their trustees on a regular basis. Naturally, part of the answer was implied by the request itself: "If you do a better job letting us know what you need, we can do more to help you get it." Another aspect was the implicit desire for better motivation -- even inspiration -- emanating from the theatres' artistic leaders.

Artistic directors appear ready to take responsibility for improved communication and for keeping boards informed and helping them learn about the artistic necessities that affect the life of the institution, the lives of the artists and the state of theatre as an art form. One of the principal duties of trustees, artistic directors feel, is to act as advocates for the theatre in the community at large. They are, most artistic directors agree, first and foremost, protectors of a theatre's idea, a theatre's work, a role they must constantly balance with their obligation to the community. They can only protect a vision they understand and believe in, however. Only when trustees are able to articulate the theatre's aesthetic can such advocacy happen.

It is therefore necessary for artistic directors to constantly (even redundantly, some feel) educate and thoroughly inform the board about aesthetic programs and choices as they are conceived and carried out. They must find ways to include trustees in advocating programming initiatives, such as a renewed commitment to producing new work or a shift to productions emphasizing directorial innovation, for example; whatever changes occur in the direction of the theatre must, some artistic directors insist, become the initiative of the board as well as the staff -- they must become part of "what we as a group, what we as a theatre are doing." Because trustees are also responsible for the fiscal health of the theatre, they are, naturally, resistant to sudden, radical changes (whereas some artists thrive on them); they also, as leaders of their communities and their businesses, naturally resist having decisions handed down to them. As a result, they must be involved in long-range planning from the beginning.

Artistic directors suggested a number of methods for improving their communication with their boards. Perhaps the most common suggestion was that more artists -- from inside or outside the company -- should be brought onto theatre boards. Whereas the artistic director's is currently the only voice articulating the theatre's artistic program, the addition of other knowledgeable voices could help clarify that program to lay trustees and help attain a balance in the dialogue between community or business and art. The opportunity for trustees to hear from playwrights, actors, designers or directors on a regular basis would help to demystify the artistic process and build trust among the theatre's governing partners. One artistic director pointed out that the inclusion of four or five artists on the board would especially benefit theatres with resident companies, giving other trustees a stronger sense of the ongoing life of the theatre. Certainly, most agree, artistic directors should have the choice whether or not to serve on the board themselves. A few artistic directors choose to stay off, believing that the theatre staff and board work best as separate but equal entities, but most choose to serve as a way of sharing the board's responsibility for the theatre. "If I'm one of them, then I can't blame them when something doesn't go my way," one artistic director explained.

Admittedly, the symbolic value of including the head of the theatre on the board is, for many artistic directors, important; just as when boards of corporations hire a chief executive officer, he or she serves on the board; so when a theatre hires an artistic leader, he or she should serve. Likewise, many artistic directors believe the managing director should sit on the board, thus ensuring representation from all three branches of the partnership. The Wilma Theater takes the symbolic a step further, passing an annual resolution confirming the independence of the artistic directors from the board in all artistic matters. And, in cases of collective artistic leadership, it is the company members themselves who constitute the majority of the board.

Artistic directors also suggested ways of strengthening communication between staffs and boards. These included: a staff person assigned to every board committee as a liaison, who would attend all meetings of that committee; all staff heads in regular attendance at board meetings; and 10-minute presentations at the beginning of each board meeting, to let the board know what is happening in some area of the theatre. Center Stage (Baltimore) has held "backstage nights," during which board members would visit all production and administrative staff members at their work posts; the staff would then make short presentations to the board members to give them a better sense of what the theatre's work is. Similarly, the Alliance Theatre (Atlanta) involves board members in specific productions. Between three and six trustees are assigned to each production. They attend production meetings, some selected rehearsals and opening night. In this way they observe the course of a production -- adopt it -- and, so, come to further understand the process. This extra participation increases the trustees' efficacy as ombudsmen for the production to the rest of the board and community. It also fuels the excitement of the Alliance trustees, who compete to participate in this popular project. Some artistic directors emphasized the importance of communicating their ideas to their boards in other exciting ways -- "wrapping packages in new ribbon" -- as part of their responsibility to keep the board inspired by and involved in the life of the theatre, and enthused about spreading the word to the rest of the community.

Boards need a larger perspective to understand the workings of their theatres. It often helps for them to see their theatre's work within the context of national theatre activity. Artistic directors acknowledge that this kind of education is their own responsibility and that they sometimes fall short of fulfilling it. Many artistic directors believe, for example, that by raising the consciousness of a board about the needs of artists countrywide, they can help that board understand the need to improve conditions for artists within their own theatre. For this reason, artistic and managing directors have regularly brought trustees to TCG National Conferences. Capital Repertory Company (Albany, N.Y.) plans four trips with its board each year to other theatres in the region. These visits, led by the artistic directors, clarify their own artistic identity within the field. The events themselves help create unity between the board and staff, while seeing other work in other institutions helps give the trustees perspective on their own theatre. A number of theatres find that outside consultants can sometimes consolidate a board in new ways. The decision to follow up on a consultant's feasibility study for a new project, for instance, becomes the board's decision; the project becomes something they are uniquely invested in, rather than being one of a series of things undertaken at the urging of the artistic director. Artistic directors suggested a number of other methods for educating trustees toward a broader national perspective, including: retreats with nationally recognized leaders in the field, visits to and from outside artistic directors, symposia with visiting theatre artists and discussions with trustees from other institutions.

As with so many of artistic directors' institutional duties, the time they spend working with their boards takes away from the time needed for the artistic work itself -- and time is the artistic resource which is most lacking. Nowhere is this drain of artistic director time more apparent than in the theatres' fund-raising efforts. Artistic directors across the country perceive that staffs of theatres are raising more and more of the theatres' money. As the costs of running theatres rise and federal funding for the arts falls off, theatres scramble to build new corporate and foundation support, and to increase individual donors through such methods as telemarketing campaigns to solicit donations from subscribers and single-ticket buyers. In addition, as one artistic director pointed out, since the decentralized noncommercial theatre began without the kind of capitalization that any other industry would consider essential, many theatres in their second or third decade of existence are only now trying to create capital in the form of endowment and artistic development funds that should have been in place initially. More and more time goes into these efforts. In addition, more and more money must be spent on the development staff necessary to raise those funds. Consequently, fund-raising departments across the country have probably experienced the biggest increases in theatre staffing, and today development directors are most often the highest-paid employees after the artistic and managing directors.

Most theatre boards have been built from theatre lovers and advocates, as well as from community leaders who offer specific expertise to the theatres' operations. Rarely, however, do theatre board members possess the kind of established wealth found on the boards of symphony orchestras and museums. These institutions have been recognized over the years as central to the culture; nonprofit theatre, a relative newcomer on the scene, has yet to gain such prestige. Whatever the reason, many artistic directors now feel they have hit the ceiling of what theatre staffs can raise as well as a ceiling on ticket prices. One artistic director suggested -- only half-joking -- a national blackout, occurring 49 percent of the way through each play performing on a nonprofit stage; at that point the show would stop and someone would tell audiences: "Unfortunately, this is all you paid for."

While virtually all artistic directors agree that their boards are an essential part of the theatres' lives, and that they could not do without them, many are troubled by the discrepancy between the time spent developing their boards and the amount of money actually raised at the board level. This imbalance has led artistic directors to explore modifications on current board structures. Many artistic directors feel that the most effective features of their current boards are the smaller, more clearly focused committees. A number of artistic directors emphasized the importance of the nominating committee and the necessity of including the artistic director in its deliberations. Likewise, long-range planning seems to many a particularly important board function, one which draws on the particular expertise of board members and involves them in the ongoing life of the theatre. As discussed, the involvement of additional artists in these proceedings is a promising modification. The reduction of board size is another type of modification possible. The Road Company (Johnson City, Tenn.) recently reduced its board from twelve members to four in order to restore the "core of energy" to the ensemble itself. The former board members were then available to be used in non-board ways, to help as they wanted to and could.

A large number of artistic directors expressed interest in the possibility of establishing advisory boards who, together with smaller, more committee-oriented boards, would take on many of the responsibilities now burdening full boards. Fund-raising efforts might be better able to attract monied patrons for participation in finite projects -- capital or endowment campaigns or real estate search committees, for example -- than for the kind of commitment required of someone joining a fulltime board. Theatres utilizing advisory groups could, artistic directors feel, draw people from all parts of the community, who would never consider or be considered to serve long-term on a board.

One aspect of the working relationship between artistic directors and boards most in need of creative exploration is the process of searching for new artistic leaders for the theatres. Artistic directors feel responsible for preparing trustees for searches, helping them identify what they want from a successor and which questions to ask potential candidates. Some theatres will want an artistic director to follow a mandate set out by founders, while others may want a strong visionary director to chart a course of his or her own. Identifying a person's aesthetic interests and creative talents is no small task, yet these are as important in an artistic director as fiscal reliability or leadership qualities. Many artistic directors believe that this exchange should begin early in the tenure of an artistic director. The first action John Hirsch took when appointed artistic director of Canada's Stratford Festival was to establish a search committee to look for his successor. Several artistic directors suggested that this kind of standing committee should be created at their own theatres to determine an organic process for identifying potential successors, meeting guest directors and seeing work at other theatres regularly. In this way boards could begin evaluating what they'll want when the time comes to find a new artistic director, and how they'll give the new leader the freedom he or she needs to lead the theatre.

Among the issues to be considered is whether an artistic director should have a contract at all, or whether, as one person suggested, a contract reduces the artistic head of the theatre to an "employee"? If so, what should the contract include for the protection of both the individual and the institution? What is the artistic director's job description? To what extent should the new artistic director have the power to restructure the theatre -- or even the board? One artistic director said he almost didn't get hired after suggesting he wanted the right to review board members, a rare prerogative for artistic directors in theatres currently. Another suggested that upon hiring a new artistic director, trustees should automatically submit their resignations, as do federal agency heads when a new President takes office. At a crucial transitional period, the act would be a symbol of respect for the artistic director's autonomy and a method of reconstituting the board to allow both for weeding out any "dead wood" and for reappointing the most productive members. Artistic directors claim that there are no definitive answers to these questions, but that each theatre must answer them individually, with the help of their current artistic director, staff, trustees, outside consultants and other experts in the field.

Artistic directors also identified a need to train prospective artistic directors to "interview theatres" more effectively in order to determine whether or not they are the right match. Often, they argue, the early stages of negotiating, once an offer has been extended, are the best times to initiate changes, but these are also the days when a new artistic director may feel least confident in asking for change, or least knowledgeable of the changes needed. For example, many believe an artistic director needs at least six months lead time to prepare for his or her first season; potential artistic directors, though, may feel that such a request will jeopardize their chances for getting the job. The tension between the leadership role of the artistic director and the tenuous position of the employee is most in evidence in these early stages, a dilemma artistic directors would like to work with their boards to ameliorate.

2. **Artistic directors need to work more effectively and responsibly with managers to ensure that business structures follow rather than precede artistic needs.**

One artistic director told the story of walking into his new job at a large regional theatre with his mind set on shrinking the institution; he was determined to cut his theatre back from the top down, paring away positions, costs and everything unnecessary, everything that didn't directly support the art. After looking over his theatre's well-oiled administration he found, to his surprise, almost nothing he felt could be eliminated, nothing that hadn't grown up to support the theatre's mission; moreover, he discovered that each staff member and virtually every dollar of every salary had been well-thought-out and hard-won. He abandoned his plan for cutting and shrinking.

The moral of the story: His respect for the theatre's management was strengthened, as was his determination to deepen the theatre's artistic resources to keep pace. Throughout the meetings, the respect artistic directors feel for the managers of their theatres was evident. In fact, most artistic directors seem to agree that the best way to help their manager-partners is to "stay out of their hair" and let them do what they do best.

Ironically, however, remaining aloof from the administration of their theatres (which they try to do wherever possible in order to focus on their own work) has resulted in concern among some artistic directors that they may be abdicating important responsibilities. In theatres involved in labor negotiations, for example, most artistic directors believe that the best time for their own participation is prior to the actual negotiating process, when optimum working conditions can still be discussed outside of the terms of a negotiating strategy. Although many artistic directors prefer to stay out of direct negotiations -- to buffer themselves from the kinds of confrontation that might jeopardize their working relationships with artists -- they are ideally suited to see both sides of most issues, since they are part of the institution, yet strongly aligned with artists at the same time. Moreover, they view it as their responsibility to ensure a proper working climate for artists. In reality, however, what one artistic director referred to as "the long-term benign neglect" of union negotiations may have reinforced a feeling of alienation between "labor and management" as opposed to creating a beneficial working climate and atmosphere of agreement between artists. Most artistic directors have never even attended such negotiations, let alone made certain that their voices have been heard during preliminary meetings; many are less familiar with the issues than they feel they should be. Whatever the issues of the moment may be, artistic directors feel in general that they must stay in closer touch with everything happening in their theatres in order to ensure that all business structures follow rather than precede artistic needs.

Even in managerial and institutional matters, the restraints artistic directors experience are located less often in their buildings or communities or partnerships than in their imaginations. They talk about the earlier years during which their theatres experienced surges of growth (as opposed to what seems like a plateau they've reached of late) as a time when almost anything seemed possible. As one artistic director said: "There are too many 'nos' now. I said more yeses when I didn't have a nickle."

The theatres they envision in the future could be structured in any of a hundred ways: Theatres could be major institutions or collectives or centers where groups of theatres share resources. They could be the brainchildren of eccentric visionaries or the jointly commanded province of leaders who rotate into the "firing line" each year or odd partnerships in which large institutions take small ones under their wings as second stages -- a theatre could be made in any image and it could reenvision itself from the inside-out, even after it got as big as the National Theatre of Great Britain. If artistic directors sent out any message in their discussions of institutional structure, it was an invitation to managers, trustees and whole communities to join them in pushing the art beyond the walls of the presently imaginable.

APPENDICES

INTERIOR WALLS: THE LIMITS OF IMAGINATION

1. Artistic Directors need time for thought, study and reflection, separate from their day-to-day producing responsibilities.

The struggles theatres face in order to survive can constrict the imaginations of those working within them; for example, the search for economical, small-cast single-set plays eliminates many artistic possibilities. Institutional functions related to the role of artistic directors as producers often directly contradict their needs as artists who direct. The continuous demand for "product" can cut deeply into time required for study and reflection. In order to concentrate on creating imaginative solutions to artistic problems, some of the things artistic directors say they need include:

-- Daily or weekly time out of the office to read and think;

-- Different sets of schedules and expectations during periods of time when they are also directing;

-- More advance time to plan projects in collaboration with other artists;

-- Additional work space that is away from that of the rest of the theatre;

-- Sabbaticals, based on the university model that enables professors to have paid leave every seven years, would aid the artistic director's longevity and diminish the potential for "burn-out."

2. Artistic directors need more consistent involvement with other artists to nourish their own creative thinking and encourage their personal visions.

Above all, artistic directors share a sense of isolation, caused by geographical distances that were created when the theatre was decentralized, as well as complex institutional structures which insulate them more and more from individual artists. They need time to:

-- See productions at other theatres;

-- Communicate with peer artistic directors;

-- Stay informed about the work of independent theatre artists.

Also contributing to the sense of isolation is the fact that most theatres have few "artistic" personnel; in fact, the artistic director is often the only fulltime artistic staff member. There is a need to deepen and expand artistic staffs nationwide, much as administrative staffs were built during the 1970s and 1980s. Some possible ways artistic directors discussed for combatting isolation both inside and outside the institution are:

-- Hiring an associate artistic director;

-- Engaging resident companies of actors;

-- Putting individual writers, designers, directors and dramaturgs on the payroll as fulltime staff members;

-- Appointing artists to serve on the board of trustees to help articulate the theatre's artistic concerns;

-- Establishing ongoing relationships with affiliated artists who have a partial time commitment to the theatre;

-- Scheduling retreats with artists and/or with artistic directors of other theatres;

-- Inviting artistic directors from other theatres as guest directors;

-- Participating in co-productions or production-sharing with other theatres.

3. Artistic Directors need more interaction with other disciplines and other fields.

Theatre artists feel isolated from the other arts and humanities; artistic directors discussed some ways of addressing this isolation by involving outside artists and experts in the lives of their theatres:

-- Committing to more collaborative projects with artists from other disciplines;

-- Adding people from other art forms or other fields to theatre staffs, boards or advisory committees;

-- Creating opportunities for field research specific to individual projects;

-- Making time for artistic directors to study in other fields, including attendance at seminars, conferences and daily time to read papers and journals;

-- Initiating symposia on topics related to the theatre's work that involve experts from outside theatrical circles;

-- Exploring connections to universities and research institutes;

-- Bringing outside experts in as advisors on specific projects;

-- Creating rehearsal processes with more time for study, research, training and viewing related material;

-- Involving people from other walks of life in research, script development, character study, audience development and other aspects of creating productions;

-- Scheduling seminars and humanities series as part of the theatre's activities.

MAKING ROOM IN THE HOUSE: LOOKING FOR NEW FLEXIBILITY IN OLD STRUCTURES

1. More flexible subscription plans and performance schedules could accommodate a variety of developmental needs and changing artistic requirements within a season.

The process of cultivating projects for the theatre is slow and variable, with each project requiring a different gestation period, but subscription deadlines can be inexorable. Consequently, seasons are viewed as things "picked" into which plays are "slotted," locking the theatre into a mode of production that lacks room for maneuvering. The following ways of adding flexibility into the season schedule were discussed by artistic directors:

-- Creating resident acting companies devoted to rotating repertory to allow for flexible playing schedules;

-- Moving a play into a second space to make room for the next production;

-- Transferring productions which can sustain additional performances to nonprofit or commercial venues;

-- Mounting tours, entering production-sharing arrangements or co-producing to allow for continued performance possibilities.

Artistic directors also believe that work suffers from insufficient time in front of an audience to continue work on discoveries made in performance. Current attitudes toward previews need to be changed. Some suggested changes include:

-- Previews should be approached as part of the rehearsal process rather than as part of the performance season;

-- Theatres need to budget for additional previews;

-- Newspapers need to be more willing to accept later deadlines for reviews;

-- Ways need to be found to keep guest artists in residence for a longer period to incorporate additional previews;

-- Rehearsal hours during previews and after opening need to be expanded;

-- Theatres could exchange rehearsal time for additional previews;

-- Audiences need to be educated about the purpose of previews, perhaps through scheduling post- and pre-show discussions.

2. More flexibility needs to be built into rehearsal schedules, so that the process is suited to the unique needs of the specific project.

There is a strong consensus that the rehearsal period contains little or no time for exploration. Changes some artistic directors would like to see in the rehearsal process include:

-- Budgeting annually for extra "swing weeks" of rehearsal to be used as needed on specific productions;

-- Pooling rehearsal time and applying time saved from one production to a longer rehearsal period for another;

-- Bringing in work from other theatres to buy rehearsal time for the theatre's own productions;

-- Maintaining the ability to juggle performing schedules throughout the season;

-- Shortening rehearsal days and spreading rehearsals out over more weeks (most artistic directors and actors would prefer five-hour days);

-- Scheduling more time for technical and dress rehearsals;

-- Rehearsing with mock-up sets;

-- Involving designers throughout the rehearsal period.

3. Methods of scheduling and programming need to be more flexible in order to accommodate a variety of projects and developmental needs.

Artistic directors want to create pipelines for work in development that might include:

-- Engaging in laboratory work with writers, actors, designers and directors that feeds the main season when work is ready;

-- Scheduling parallel seasons in alternative spaces throughout the theatre's community;

-- Hiring artists who bring their own projects to develop at the theatre;

-- Encouraging designers to initiate projects;

-- Maintaining fully staffed workshops separate from the production season;

-- Budgeting funds specifically to commission playwrights and other creators;

-- Channeling new or unexpected money from popular successes directly into future artistic development;

-- Increasing artistic staffs devoted entirely to ongoing developmental projects;

-- Co-producing or scheduling subsequent productions of the same play as a means of furthering developmental projects;

-- Developing work in three- or four-stage workshops to identify potential projects for future seasons;

-- Participating in artistic director retreats or think-tanks for season planning;

-- Hiring a variety of artists as consultants for the planning of a season.

THINKING BEYOND FOUR WALLS: THE INDIVIDUAL ARTIST AS A NATIONAL PRIORITY

The single most pressing concern for the majority of artistic directors is to find ways of keeping the most talented artists in the theatre, as television and film continue to offer extraordinary celebrity and compensation.

1. Artistic directors are concerned with keeping artists in the theatre; they need to constantly renew their commitment to making their theatres homes for artists.

Artists need to feel more at home in the theatres, less like hired hands brought in to fulfill a function and then move on. Some of the solutions currently being explored are:

-- Creating a more supportive environment for artists, designed to suit individual needs and working methods, and to involve them in the theatre's ongoing life, such as private work space with necessary office equipment for directors and playwrights, and time for work and reflection;

71

-- Providing convenient and attractive housing for guest artists, equipped with furniture, telephones, television, even fresh flowers;

-- Actively welcoming artists into the theatre community by greeting them at train stations or airports, organizing group parties, hiring company managers sympathetic to the needs of artists, and encouraging volunteer groups to create their own methods for making guest artists feel at home.

2. Theatres and artists alike need to find creative ways to address the chronic undercompensation in the field.

Artistic directors are deeply concerned with the broad issues of compensation and are unanimous about the fact that nonprofit theatres do not yet pay artists enough. Some of the complex facets of this far-reaching problem include:

-- Artists express deep frustration at not being able to make a living or maintain a life while doing the work they love in the theatre;

-- Artists increasingly view theatre as a young person's profession for people under 40 whose financial responsibilities are modest;

-- Theatres are troubled by the difficulty of getting and keeping commitments from actors;

-- Geography and distance work against theatres located away from the commercial production centers where actors feel they need to be based to have access to other work;

-- Theatres are torn between their desire to see actors take advantage of lucrative opportunities in the media and the impulse to be more forceful in demanding that contracts and commitments be honored. Artistic directors blame themselves for complicity in this dynamic because they don't always demonstrate a strong enough commitment to the actor to be able to expect the actor to commit to them;

-- The disintegration of the resident acting ensemble of the '60s and '70s may have reinforced a feeling of insecurity on the part of actors entering the profession;

-- While a growing number of artistic directors are attracted to the goal of creating resident companies, most agree that the current economics of theatre conspire against permanent ensembles of sufficient size.

Some of the ways artistic directors discussed to help create a livelihood for artists include:

-- Employing more artists -- playwrights, directors, designers and actors -- on a year-round basis, and finding ways to budget salaries for fulltime resident artists that are commensurate with those offered to faculty members of academic institutions;

-- Setting the goal of raising fees for guest artists as part of long-range planning;

-- Exploring new incentives for artists to choose work in theatre over higher paying work in film and television, such as by establishing and maintaining exciting collaborations among artists;

-- Taking collective action whereby a group of theatres pool resources to support a writer, director or designer on a year-round salaried basis;

-- Creating new structures for larger, looser networks of artists than are currently defined as "ensembles," including efforts community-wide and nationally for theatres to band together to provide continued support and employment for artists;

-- Reevaluating compensation arrangements for playwrights, possibly combining fees for time in residence with royalties and commissions;

-- Encouraging larger institutions with more resources to increase salaries as much as possible in order to allow artists to also accept work at smaller theatres with fewer financial resources;

-- Finding other ways to compensate artists for work in the theatre, such as paying a playwright a separate fee for attending rehearsals;

-- Seeking outside paid employment for actors -- commercial work, voice-overs, teaching, docent tours, advertising connections -- to supplement their salaries and connect them with the community;

-- Finding ways to reduce the number of projects directors and designers must accept in order to support themselves.

3. Theatres need to build better long-term relationships with artists and find ways of integrating them into the ongoing life of the institutions.

Efforts to involve more artists with theatres in a continuing way and to include more of their spiritual presence in artistic policy-making include:

-- New attempts to create resident acting ensembles in theatres where the presence of a permanent company makes aesthetic sense and helps overcome the difficulty of hiring them show-by-show, and to find ways of keeping such ensembles growing in size and quality;

-- Programs for training resident actors; for example, through retreats, ongoing classes and workshops, master classes with guest artists and senior artists becoming mentors for younger ones;

-- Creation of advisory committees, holding regular meetings between actors and management, and introducing guest actors to the complete staff;

-- Additional staff positions for artists, including associate artistic directors, residencies and associate artist positions for writers, directors and designers;

-- Longer and earlier involvement of artists in individual projects;

-- Involvement of the artists in the life of the local community;

-- Providing artistic challenges such as encouraging actors to stretch and experiment through playing a variety of parts;

-- Developing systems of providing local, regional and national recognition, especially for mature talent and senior independent artists;

-- Rewarding stages of advancement and providing opportunities for promotion, as in ballet companies, where artists proceed from the corps through several stages to principal dancer;

-- Finding ways to increase the visibility of actors and other artists, for example by touring productions or transferring them to other theatres, and by encouraging the press to celebrate the achievements of theatre artists;

-- Establishing ways to honor and recognize experience, achievement and continued service of artists.

4. There is a need to invest in the future of the art form and the profession by taking responsibility for the training of and access for future artists and nontraditional artists, including minority and women artists.

Something serious is lacking in the training of American theatre artists, artistic directors agree, and most of today's graduates do not aspire to careers on the stage. The conduit between training programs and professional theatres has been severed, and many young artists, particularly actors, no longer meet the craft demands of stage performance. Some possible ways artistic directors feel they might address the situation are:

-- Becoming directly involved in training programs and making concerted attempts to reestablish bonds between universities and the profession, including efforts to identify excellent teachers and to create training that inspires students to want careers in theatre;

-- Improving access for young artists entering the theatre through earlier scouting, and opportunities for work and observation;

-- Sending a clear message to training institutions concerning the kinds of training required for an artist to make a life in the theatre;

-- Strengthening connections between university programs and theatres by creating more apprenticeships, internships, new affiliations between teaching programs within the theatres, contracts for seasonal work for students graduating from training programs run by other nonprofit theatres and second companies within theatres for young professionals.

Artistic directors also believe that they have generally done far too little to promote and provide access for minority, ethnic and women artists. In order to provide more such opportunities, they discussed the following:

-- Opening theatres to more diverse artists who reflect our racially mixed, interdependent world;

-- Looking at the ethnic and gender composition of play casts in new and imaginative ways;

-- Making a commitment to produce plays that draw on the experiences of many cultures and races.

OUR AUDIENCE OURSELVES

The responsibility artistic directors feel toward their audiences creates one of the more pressing questions they face: how to strike a balance between their own artistic challenges and the pressure to fill the theatre with a satisfied audience. They look for ways to overcome a sense of alienation from their audiences and from the people who aren't attending the theatre at all.

1. <u>Artistic directors want to expand theatre audiences to include members of the community who don't traditionally subscribe and those who rarely attend, without jeopardizing their personal artistic visions.</u>

Many artistic directors fear they rely too heavily on a single, fairly
homogeneous audience, usually subscribers, who tend to be white, middle-
class, educated, over 45, raised on theatregoing, financially secure and
possessing a propensity towards advance planning. As this subscription
group ages, artistic directors worry that they see no new generations of
subscribers; they also lament the fact that their audience does not more
clearly reflect the demographics of society. The audience they want is
made up of many audiences.

Some of the ideas theatres have tried in order to develop and expand
their audiences include:

 -- Reducing the number of offerings in a subscription plan to make
    it more affordable and to decrease the required time commitment;

 -- Co-producing or mounting regional tours to engage in contact
    with larger or different audiences;

 -- Building audiences through a renewed commitment to a personal
    vision and finding the specific audience for that work;

 -- Cultivating minority audiences through a demonstrated commitment
    to make the theatre relevant to ethnic and minority communities
    through nontraditional casting initiatives, consistent
    programming of the work of minority artists, booking in touring
    productions of important plays by ethnic artists and outreach
    marketing methods developed with a sensitivity to the specific
    needs of non-theatregoing communities;

 -- Creating flexible memberships or passes as an alternative -- or
    supplement -- to subscriptions, for those who do not want to
    commit far in advance;

 -- Conducting research to determine why people don't attend theatre
    and how to get them into the theatre;

 -- Lowering ticket prices and developing more adventurous pricing
    schemes for discounted tickets to bring in price-sensitive and
    young audiences, such as rush or half-price tickets on the day
    of performance, and low-cost standing room tickets.

2. Theatres need to take the initiative to develop and educate future
audiences.

Most artistic directors look for tomorrow's audience in today's
classroom, and most theatres have some type of outreach programming.
Some of the programs currently addressing this future audience include:

 -- Performances for school audiences such as regular student
    matinees at the theatre, apprentice and second company
    productions for young audiences and touring productions to the
    schools;

-- Tours of the theatre's facilities for young people, led by the artists;

-- Discount or free ticket programs for students and for children who bring their parents and other family members;

-- Theatre techniques used to teach courses in other disciplines;

-- Workshops for teachers;

-- Programs that educate children about theatre and make it relevant to their lives, including involvement with special groups such as juvenile court programs, the handicapped or drug abusers;

-- Plays commissioned specifically for student or young audiences;

-- Plays developed through collaborations between professionals and young people.

RENOVATING THE ROOM AT THE TOP

Many theatres have blossomed into major institutions housed in buildings held in trust by boards and operated with increasingly sophisticated management systems. Many have recently undergone changes in artistic leadership. Most are in need of new levels of financial, legal and political support. These factors have transformed what began largely as small companies of artists to companies predominated by administrators. The duties of artistic directors have grown more demanding and complex, and a new partnership has arisen among artists, managers and trustees. Many artistic directors are troubled by a bottom-line mentality on the part of trustees that sometimes takes precedence over artistic concerns, as well as a discrepancy between the time they spend working with their boards and the amount of money actually raised at the board level. Nevertheless, artistic directors agree that their boards are essential and that they could not do without them.

1. Artistic directors need to communicate more effectively with their boards of trustees and work with them to reevaluate board structures, and to make sure these structures serve the artistic mission, especially in theatres with new artistic directors and longer-lived trustees.

Some of the steps that artistic directors discussed to improve communication and working relationships with their trustees were:

-- Bringing more artists onto the theatre's board to supplement the artistic director's voice and help balance the dialogue between business and art;

77

-- Ensuring that artistic directors have the choice of whether or not to serve on the board;

-- Strengthening communication between staffs and boards through such mechanisms as assigning a staff person as liaison to every board committee, ensuring regular department head attendance at board meetings to make presentations on the activities of various areas of the theatre's operations;

-- Involving trustees as observers during the rehearsal process;

-- Providing opportunities for board members to interact with playwrights, directors, designers and actors to demystify the artistic process;

-- Giving trustees a context for their perceptions about their theatres by informing them of national theatre trends and issues;

-- Taking trustees to see work at other theatres;

-- Planning regular board retreats, perhaps involving recognized artists, other artistic directors, national leaders in the field and other trustees;

-- Exploring modifications on current board structures, such as creating an advisory committee to handle some of the work currently assigned to the full board;

-- Preparing trustees in advance for the process of searching for new artistic directors by establishing a standing search committee, providing the committee with access to guest directors, encouraging them to see work regularly at other theatres and introducing them to outside consultants.

2. Artistic directors need to work more effectively and responsibly with managers to ensure that business structures follow rather than precede artistic needs.

Throughout the meetings, the respect artistic directors feel for their managers was evident. Yet many artistic directors feel that this respect has sometimes kept them aloof from the theatre's administration and may have caused them to abdicate important responsibilities. Two ways artistic directors feel would help them keep better informed are:

-- Holding meetings with managing directors well in advance of union negotiations to prioritize artistic needs and concerns;

-- Participating regularly in meetings with other artistic directors from theatres nationwide to keep informed of issues affecting their own theatres and the national theatre community.

ABOUT THE PROJECT

The Artistic Home is a report on the series of nationwide meetings with the American theatre's artistic directors, convened as part of TCG's National Artistic Agenda Project. The multifaceted project, launched in the spring of 1987 with the support of special grants from the Dayton Hudson Foundation, the National Endowment for the Arts and the Pew Charitable Trusts, has to date included seven regional meetings of artistic directors followed by six meetings of smaller task forces, and four regional roundtables of unaffiliated theatre artists. The regional meetings, hosted by theatres in New Haven, Baltimore, New York City, Chicago, Atlanta, Los Angeles and San Francisco, brought together more than 120 artistic directors to participate in wide-ranging discussions of the artistic resources needed in order for the American theatre to achieve its artistic potential.

Conceived as an exploration and a dialogue, the National Artistic Agenda Project did not seek any simple or uniform prescriptions, but aimed to develop a tool for each theatre to address its specific artistic needs in its own way, beginning an ambitious, ongoing education program for artists, managers and trustees that would allow serious, qualitative consideration of the theatre's artistic mission. TCG hoped the project could engender an understanding of both national and individual theatre needs, by providing visibility for universally experienced problems, as well as incorporating the potential for localized utilization and supplementation by each individual theatre.

Based on comments and concerns solicited in advance from TCG's 220 Constituent theatres and recommendations from the TCG board of directors, participants were asked to discuss ways to increase artistic resources, consider whether current working methods are serving the art form and entertain alternative structures that might better serve the noncommercial theatre. The agenda for each meeting was identical and designed for maximum flexibility, creating a springboard for each artistic director to think about his or her needs as an artistic director, and the artistic goals of the institution.

TCG director Peter Zeisler encouraged the participants to approach the discussions of artistic ideals, goals and dreams from "zero-based" thinking: "If we could start over and recreate the nonprofit theatre as if anything were possible, how would we do it?" Participants were asked to put aside questions of finances and to address primary artistic needs without regard to their cost. Specific agenda topics dealt with creative process, artists, repertoire, audiences and structure/practices. The participants discussed these areas from three points of view: the ideal, obstacles/problems and creative solutions/alternatives.

Parallel to the regional meetings, TCG convened a similar series of meetings of unaffiliated artists in New York, Chicago and San Francisco as part of its ongoing Artist Roundtable series. These meetings, which included freelance directors, designers, actors and playwrights, were separate from the National Artistic Agenda Project, but provided useful perspectives for this report from theatre professionals who are not permanently based at institutions.

Following the regional artistic director meetings, smaller task forces of four-to-six artistic directors met to address the issues raised at each of the larger meetings, and to explore more fully creative solutions to overcoming problems. The task forces began to hammer out the issues that would become the basis for this report.

Written by consultant Todd London, who attended all 17 meetings around the country, The Artistic Home is intended to capture the spirit of the discussions by articulating the divergent and common concerns of artistic directors on a variety of topics which affect the professional theatre as a whole. It also sets forth some of the thousands of ideas expressed, and includes examples of the ways individual theatres have overcome specific problems and stimulated creative work.

The Artistic Home will be distributed to artistic directors, managers and trustees of all TCG constituent theatres, and is available for purchase by the public. The National Artistic Agenda Project will continue, bringing these questions before the profession at the upcoming TCG National Conference in June 1988, where managing directors, trustees and individual artists will again be brought into the discussion. The TCG board of directors is currently considering other ways to extend the impact of the project into the future by creating an ongoing dialogue about the artistic health of America's theatre.

REGIONAL ARTISTIC DIRECTOR MEETINGS

New Haven, Conn.

March 2, 1987
Host:
Yale Repertory Theatre
Lloyd Richards, Artistic Director

Baltimore, Md.

March 16, 1987
Host:
Center Stage
Stan Wojewodski, Jr., Artistic Director

New York, N.Y.

March 30, 1987
Host:
McCarter Theatre
Nagle Jackson, Artistic Director

Chicago, Ill.

April 6, 1987
Host:
Goodman Theatre
Robert Falls, Artistic Director

Atlanta, Ga.

April 27, 1987
Host:
Alliance Theatre
Robert Farley, Artistic Director

Los Angeles, Calif.

May 4, 1987
Host:
Mark Taper Forum
Gordon Davidson, Artistic Director

Berkeley, Calif.

May 28, 1987
Hosts:
Berkeley Repertory Theatre
Sharon Ott, Artistic Director
Eureka Theatre
Anthony Taccone, Artistic Director

TASK FORCE MEETINGS

New Haven, Conn.	March 3, 1987
Baltimore, Md.	March 16, 1987
New York, N.Y.	March 31, 1987
Chicago, Ill.	April 7, 1987
Los Angeles, Calif.	May 5, 1987
San Francisco, Calif.	May 29, 1987

NATIONAL ARTISTIC AGENDA PROJECT

Lindy Zesch, Project Director

Todd London, Project Consultant

Nancy Walther, Executive Assistant

ABOUT TCG

Theatre Communications Group is the national service organization for the nonprofit professional theatre. Since its founding in 1961, TCG has developed a unique and comprehensive support system that addresses the artistic and management concerns of theatres, as well as institutionally based and freelance artists nationwide.

TCG provides a national forum and communications network for a field that is as aesthetically diverse as it is geographically widespread. Its goals are to foster the cross-fertilization of ideas among the individuals and institutions comprising the profession; to improve the artistic and administrative capabilities of the field; to enhance the visibility and demonstrate the achievements of the American theatre by increasing public awareness of the theatre's role in society; and to encourage the development of a mutually supportive network of professional companies and artists that collectively represent our "national theatre."

TCG's more than 30 centralized services and programs facilitate the work of thousands of actors, artistic and managing directors, playwrights, literary managers, directors, designers, trustees and administrative personnel, as well as a constituency of more than 275 theatre institutions across the country.

TCG gratefully acknowledges its individual contributors, as well as the following corporations, foundations and government agencies for their generous support:

Actors' Equity Foundation; Alcoa Foundation; Atlantic Richfield Foundation; AT&T Foundation; Citicorp/Citibank; Columbia Pictures Industries; Consolidated Edison Company of New York; Consulate General of Spain; The Eleanor Naylor Dana Charitable Trust; Dayton Hudson Foundation; Exxon Corporation; The William and Mary Greve Foundation; Home Box Office; Japan-United States Friendship Commission; The Andrew W. Mellon Foundation; Mobil Foundation; National Broadcasting Company; National Endowment for the Arts; New York Life Foundation; New York State Council on the Arts; The Pew Charitable Trusts; Philip Morris, Inc.; The Rockefeller Foundation; The Scherman Foundation; Shell Companies Foundation; The Shubert Foundation; Xerox Foundation.

Josephine R. Abady, Artistic Director, Berkshire Theatre Festival, Stockbridge, Mass.

Abigail Adams, Associate Artistic Director, The People's Light and Theatre Company, Malvern, Penn.

*Eve Adamson, Artistic Director, Jean Cocteau Repertory, New York, N.Y.

Peter Altman, Producing Director, Huntington Theatre Company, Boston, Mass.

Vincent Anthony, Executive Director, Center for Puppetry Arts, Atlanta, Ga.

Clinton J. Atkinson, Artistic Director, Long Island Stage, Hempstead, N.Y.

Luis Barroso, Director, Performance Program, Center for Puppetry Arts, Atlanta, Ga.

William J. Becvar, Artistic Director, Tacoma Actors Guild, Tacoma, Wash.

Martin Benson, Artistic Director, South Coast Repertory, Costa Mesa, Calif.

Tanya Berezin, Interim Artistic Director, Circle Repertory Company, New York, N.Y.

Conrad Bishop, Artistic Director, The Independent Eye, Lancaster, Penn.

*Margaret Booker, Artistic Director, The Hartman Theatre, Stamford, Conn.

*Bruce Bouchard, Producing Director, Capital Repertory Company, Albany, N.Y.

Gregory Boyd, Artistic Director, StageWest, Springfield, Mass.

Amie Brockway, Artistic Director, The Open Eye: New Stagings, New York, N.Y.

Arvin Brown, Artistic Director, Long Wharf Theatre, New Haven, Conn.

Pat Brown, Artistic/Executive Director, Alley Theatre, Houston, Tex.

Bill Bushnell, Artistic Producing Director, Los Angeles Theatre Center, Los Angeles, Calif.

Larry Carpenter, Artistic Director, American Stage Festival, Milford, N.H.

*Tisa Chang, Artistic/Producing Director, Pan Asian Repertory Theatre, New York, N.Y.

Jill Charles, Artistic Director, Dorset Theatre Festival, Dorset, Vt.

Peter H. Clough, Producing Director, Capital Repertory Company, Albany, N.Y.

Frank Condon, Associate Artistic Director, Odyssey Theatre Ensemble, Los Angeles, Calif.

Gayle Cornelison, General Director, California Theatre Center, Sunnyvale, Calif.

James Crabtree, Producing Director, Cumberland County Playhouse, Crossville, Tenn.

Jon Cranney, Artistic Director, The Children's Theatre Company, Minneapolis, Minn.

*Gordon Davidson, Artistic Director/Producer, Mark Taper Forum, Los Angeles, Calif.

*John Dillon, Artistic Director, Milwaukee Repertory Theater, Milwaukee, Wisc.

Olympia Dukakis, Producing Artistic Director, Whole Theatre, Montclair, N.J.

*David Emmes, Producing Artistic Director, South Coast Repertory,
   Costa Mesa, Calif.

Robert Egan, Resident Director, Mark Taper Forum, Los Angeles,
   Calif.

*Robert Falls, Artistic Director, Goodman Theatre, Chicago, Ill.

Robert Farley, Artistic Director, Alliance Theatre, Atlanta, Ga.

Michael Fields, Co-Artistic Director, Dell'Arte Players Company, Blue
   Lake, Calif.

Donald Forrest, Co-Artistic Director, Dell'Arte Players Company, Blue
   Lake, Calif.

*David Frank, Artistic Director, Studio Arena Theatre, Buffalo, N.Y.

Gerald Freedman, Artistic Director, Great Lakes Theater Festival,
   Cleveland, Ohio

William T. Gardner, Producing Director, Pittsburgh Public Theater,
   Pittsburgh, Penn.

Moses Goldberg, Producing Director, Stage One: The Louisville
   Children's Theatre, Louisville, Ky.

Edward J. Gryska, Artistic Director, The Salt Lake Acting Company,
   Salt Lake City, Utah

Warren Hammack, Director, Horse Cave Theatre, Horse Cave, Ky.

David Hammond, Artistic Director, PlayMakers Repertory Company, Chapel
   Hill, N.C.

Jay Harnick, Artistic Director, Theatreworks/USA, New York, N.Y.

Bernard Havard, Executive Director, The Walnut Street Theatre,
   Philadelphia, Penn.

*Edward R. Hastings, Artistic Director, American Conservatory Theatre,
   San Francisco, Calif.

Patrick Henry, Producer/Artistic Director, Free Street Theater,
   Chicago, Ill.

Joan Holden, Member, San Francisco Mime Troupe, San Francisco, Calif.

Richard Hopkins, Artistic Director, Florida Studio Theatre, Sarasota, Fla.

*Elizabeth Huddle, Artistic Director, Intiman Theatre Company, Seattle, Wash.

Gregory S. Hurst, Producing Director, Pennsylvania Stage Company, Allentown, Penn.

*Nagle Jackson, Artistic Director, McCarter Theatre, Princeton, N.J.

Douglas Jacobs, Artistic Director, San Diego Repertory Theatre, San Diego, Calif.

Jon Jory, Producing Director, Actors Theatre of Louisville, Louisville, Ky.

Steve Kaplan, Artistic Director, Manhattan Punch Line, New York, N.Y.

Michael Kahn, Artistic Director, The Acting Company, New York, N.Y. and Shakespeare Theatre at the Folger, Washington, D.C.

*John Kauffman, Artistic Director, Honolulu Theatre for Youth, Honolulu, Hi.

*George Keathley, Artistic Director, Missouri Repertory Theatre, Kansas City, Mo.

Eric Krebs, Producing Director, George Street Playhouse, New Brunswick, N.J.

*Mark Lamos, Artistic Director, Hartford Stage Company, Hartford, Conn.

Robert H. Leonard, Producing Director, The Road Company, Johnson City, Tenn.

Simon L. Levy, Artistic Director, One Act Theatre Company of San Francisco, San Francisco, Calif.

John Lion, General Director, Magic Theatre, San Francisco, Calif.

*Susan Albert Loewenberg, Producing Director, L.A. Theatre Works, Los Angeles, Calif.

Theodore Mann, Artistic Director, Circle in the Square Theatre, New York, N.Y.

Tom Markus, Artistic Director, Theatre by the Sea, Portsmouth, N.H.

Donovan Marley, Artistic Director, Denver Center Theatre Company, Denver, Col.

Des McAnuff, Artistic Director, La Jolla Playhouse, La Jolla, Calif.

*Lynne Meadow, Artistic Director, Manhattan Theatre Club, New York, N.Y.

Allan Miller, Co-Producing Director, The Back Alley Theatre, Van Nuys, Calif.

Howard J. Millman, Producing Director, Geva Theatre, Rochester, N.Y.

Arnold Mittelman, Producing Artistic Director, Coconut Grove Playhouse, Miami, Fla.

Charles Morey, Artistic Director, Pioneer Theatre Company, Salt Lake City, Utah

Cleveland Morris, Artistic Director, Delaware Theatre Company, Wilmington, Del.

Bonnie Morris, Producing Director, Illusion Theater, Minneapolis, Minn.

Timothy Near, Interim Artistic Director, San Jose Repertory Company, San Jose, Calif.

Jack O'Brien, Artistic Director, Old Globe Theatre, San Diego, Calif.

*Sharon Ott, Artistic Director, Berkeley Repertory Theatre, Berkeley, Calif.

Tina Packer, Artistic Director, Shakespeare & Company, Lenox, Mass.

William Partlan, Artistic Director, The Cricket Theatre, Minneapolis, Minn.

Jean Passanante, Artistic Director, New York Theatre Workshop, New York, N.Y.

Joan Patchen, Executive Director, The Playwrights' Center, Minneapolis, Minn.

Carey Perloff, Artistic Director, CSC Repertory Ltd. - The Classic Stage Company, New York, N.Y.

Jane Reid-Petty, Producing Director, New Stage Theatre, Jackson, Miss.

Gregory Poggi, Producing Director, Philadephia Drama Guild, Philadelphia, Penn.

James P. Reber, Executive Producer, San Jose Repertory Company, San Jose, Calif.

*Lloyd Richards, Artistic Director, Yale Repertory Theatre, New Haven, Conn. and O'Neill Theater Center National Playwrights Conference, Waterford, Conn.

Michael Robins, Producing Director, Illusion Theater, Minneapolis, Minn.

Carol Rocamora, Artistic/Producing Director, Philadelphia Festival Theatre for New Plays, Philadelphia, Penn.

*Barbara Rosoff, Artistic Director, Portland Stage Company, Portland, Me.

Phyllis Jane Rose, Artistic Director, At the Foot of the Mountain, Minneapolis, Minn.

D. Nicholas Rudall, Artistic Director, Court Theatre, Chicago, Ill.

Jerry Russell, Artistic/Managing Director, Stage West, Fort Worth, Tex.

Lawrence Sacharow, Artistic Director, River Arts Repertory, Woodstock, N.Y.

Daniel L. Schay, Producing Director, Merrimack Repertory Theatre, Lowell, Mass.

Joan Schirle, Co-Artistic Director, Dell'Arte Players Company, Blue Lake, Calif.

Ted Schmitt, Producing Artistic Director, The CAST Theatre, Hollywood, Calif.

*Lawrence E. Sloan, Artistic Director, Remains Theatre, Chicago, Ill.

Gray Smith, Executive Director, The Street Theater, White Plains, N.Y.

Marc P. Smith, Executive Producer/Artistic Director, Worcester Foothills Theatre Company, Worcester, Mass.

Robert Smyth, Artistic Director, Lamb's Players Theatre, National City, Calif.

Ron Sossi, Artistic Director, Odyssey Theatre Ensemble, Los Angeles, Calif.

Jeff Steitzer, Resident Director, A Contemporary Theatre, Seattle, Wash.

Arthur Storch, Producing Artistic Director, Syracuse Stage, Syracuse, N.Y.

*Daniel Sullivan, Artistic Director, Seattle Repertory Theatre, Seattle, Wash.

J.R. Sullivan, Producing Director, New American Theater, Rockford, Ill.

Marlene Swartz, Co-Artistic Director, Soho Repertory Theatre, New York, N.Y.

*Fontaine Syer, Artistic Director, Theatre Project Company, St. Louis, Mo.

*Anthony Taccone, Artistic Director, Eureka Theatre Company, San Francisco, Calif.

*Charles Towers, Artistic Director, Virginia Stage Company, Norfolk, Va.

Jerry Turner, Artistic Director, Oregon Shakepearean Festival, Ashland, Ore.

*Russell Vandenbroucke, Artistic Director, Northlight Theatre, Evanston, Ill.

Douglas Wager, Associate Producing Director, Arena Stage, Washington, D. C.

Leonard T. Wagner, Co-Producing Director, Chocolate Bayou Theater Company, Houston, Tex.

Frank Wittow, Producing Artistic Director, Academy Theatre, Atlanta, Ga.

*Stan Wojewodski, Jr., Artistic Director, Center Stage, Baltimore, Md.

Sam Woodhouse, Producing Director, San Diego Repertory Theatre, San Diego, Calif.

Steven Woolf, Artistic Director, The Repertory Theatre of St. Louis, Mo.

Michael T. Yeager, Producing and Artistic Director, Snowmass Repertory Theatre, Snowmass Village, Col.

Dennis Zacek, Artistic Director, Victory Gardens Theater, Chicago, Ill.

Joy Zinoman, Artistic and Managing Director, The Studio Theatre, Washington, D.C.

*Jiri Zizka, Artistic/Executive Director, The Wilma Theatre, Philadelphia, Penn.

*Denotes Task Force Member

92

NOTES